MWAA630289

TESTIMONIALS

"Laura is living proof and an exemplar, of someone who has been very far into the darkness, and has come back. She is therefore a very credible person with whom to explore this new way of relating to money, prosperity, safety, security and control. She is credible in ways that most simply are not."

Barnet Bain
Author
Producer, What Dreams May Come,
Director, Milton's Secret with Eckhart Tolle

"Words have no power to describe what I felt and saw, when reading this book. This is the owner's manual that humans are looking for and is incredibly powerful energy and information, and Laura's craft is flawless. This is the knowledge that every human is looking for and should be presented at birth."

Jessie Morgan
Spiritual Teacher

"Laura's 'Priceless' teachings on true wealth and true worth tap into the ultimate zeitgeist of our times, exposing the false concepts that have kept us trapped in limitation, hypnotized by the belief that our source is outside of us — and giving us a path back home again. A path back to our true value, our true abundance, and the power to manifest our purpose and potential beyond what we have imagined! As my coach and guide many times, I can't even begin to put a price on what she's given to my life."

Derek Rydall
Best Selling Author

"Laura has had experiences that would surely have destroyed many people; and has utilized these experiences as a powerful catalyst for transformation within herself. Now she is sharing this transformation in an easy path that anyone can follow. Her work is sure to help millions of people remember their self love and personal power."

James Barnard
Founder, Mandala Growth Partners

"Through working with Laura, I've come into a relationship with myself in a new way and discovered how to "flip the script" on the mindsets that were sabotaging me. Laura has guided me with compassion and wisdom, providing me with a roadmap when I felt lost in drama and chaos. Laura has a profound gift for elevating people to become the most fulfilled versions of themselves and I am deeply grateful for her work."

Abby Epstein
Film Director

"Laura's words and wisdom travel far beyond what anyone can imagine. Her teachings resonate on a spiritual & vibrational level that cause major positive effects in each person she shares with, and every person they share with from that point on. You have impacted my life greatly and I have been applying your help to everyone I meet."

Natalia Zeltzer
Founder, Be Real Ibiza

"In a world seemingly over-saturated with self help and diluted spiritually. I crave Laura's honest reflections. They pack a certain punch and I think the best word to describe her offerings is genuine, raw and real."

Anthony Berlingeri
Yoga, Meditation and Mindfulness Guide

A JOURNEY BACK TO SELF

FOR THOSE WHO HAVE LOST THEIR WAY

Written by

Laura Fredrickson

A JOURNEY BACK TO SELF
For Those Who Have Lost Their Way

Copyright © 2021 by Laura Fredrickson

All rights reserved. No part of this publication may be reproduced, distributed or transmitted in any form or by any means, including photocopying, recording, or other electronic or mechanical methods, without the written permission of Laura Fredrickson, except in the case of brief quotations embodied in critical reviews and specific other noncommercial uses permitted by copyright law.

ISBN: 978-1-7378084-1-1

Cover design: Laura Fredrickson
Photograph back cover: Precilia de Carvalho
Layout design: Lazar Kackarovski

To my parents Paul and Jean,
and to all who lost their way.

TABLE OF CONTENTS

SECTION ONE
YOUR JOURNEY BACK TO SELF

SECTION TWO
WINGING IT INNERVIEWS

FOREWORD

*A*t one point or another on life's long journey, many of us will grapple with the experience of becoming lost. Our sense of identity may be upended by losing a longtime career or position, letting go of a cherished friend or family member, or we may be faced with an unexpected health crisis or a major financial loss. Whatever the cause, this becoming lost can pull our reference points right out from underneath us, leaving us despairing and disoriented.

Like a child in the darkening forest, our best hope at such a time is to find some way back to a place that makes sense to us, a place where the way forward becomes visible once again. And to find that place, we need some sign or symbol or reminder left by another who has been where we are once or twice and has found their way back to safety. In short, we need *breadcrumbs* that we can begin to follow from one to the other, even in the darkest hour.

Laura Fredrickson is such a person; one who has lived through the death of both her parents through suicide, ruinous financial losses in the dot com collapse, and the loss of deep love in relationship.

More importantly, she is one who found her way through each of these destabilizing life challenges towards a deeper resiliency and a greater flourishing. And to our benefit, she had the presence of mind to take notes along the way, recording her learnings and molding them into straightforward explanations and processes to help others navigating similar territory.

What you will find in this volume is not simply words or notions, but breadcrumbs. The chapters herein are designed to help you find your way back to yourself, when you find yourself lost in life's many twists and turns.

However this came about, however suddenly or gradually, the crumbs laid down here by Laura and others who have faced devastating loss and challenge, can be a vital resource in remembering your way homeward.

On the path of life we all find ourselves turned around from time to time, and sometimes we wander off the trail entirely or fall off a hidden ledge and find ourselves in need of real help. In this book, Laura has worked diligently to assemble an emergency kit — with a compress for a broken heart, a map of what really matters and what leads us astray, and a moral compass pointing the way on our crucial journey back to Self.

May it serve you in your time of need, and inspire you when your feet are back on the Way.

—Benjamin Francis Phelan

PREFACE

*F*or those of you that are feeling depressed, discouraged and powerless, please know that you are not alone. It's okay to not be okay. We have all been there. No one is exempt! It is part of the human plight and journey. This too shall pass.

If you are considering ending your life, rest assured that countless others have experienced this same intensity of despair. There is no judgment and no shame for the depths of what you are feeling and considering.

There is an invitation however to recognize that what is wanting to die, has nothing to do with your physical body. If the choice to take your own life should arise within you, know that it is governed by your limited mind. If you can listen to the whisper of your soul, you will discover true liberation.

Please know that these words that you are receiving now, are imbued with a deep warm angelic embrace, with so much love and honor for your courageous journey.

This book is intended as a sacred prayer for you to hold, as a reflection of the sacred prayer that is *you*. This is an owners manual for your magnificence.

These reflections and reminders are the language of your soul, whispered softly to evoke within you a deep reverence of your innate worth and your signature significance to this planet.

This is a banquet of morsels and food for thought - delectable cuisine, marinated in love and infused with soulular nutrition. The invitation is to digest at your own pace for your embodied integration. As with any journey, it is important to have 'rest stops' to allow yourself time to breathe, receive, digest and marinate.

All that is being shared is not new information, but rather reminders of your innate wisdom. The degree of which you have migrated from these core truths is up for loving and compassionate discovery.

This is a knowing that is encoded within your DNA, beckoning to be unlocked by your conscious realization of your own beauty and divinity. Each word is inviting and welcoming a greater coherence and unity with your essential awe-full Self.

CLARIFIER

*T*he terms Source, God, Spirit, Divine, Infinite Intelligence and Creator (as well as others), represent the benevolent energy that is permeating our existence, and exists within all beings.

Finding words to encompass such vast wisdom, immense orchestration and the majesty of this existence, may be futile.

This loving energy and the infinite resource of source is the undercurrent of life—from the macrocosm to the microcosm, spanning the furthest reaches of the Universe, to the intimate details of your cells.

PROLOGUE

n all great ages of times past, accounts of prolific heroes are found.

Tales are told of incredibly courageous human beings, who challenged the powers to be and catalyzed great change for the next chapter of human evolution.

This time is no different, but with an important and life changing distinction.

We are no longer writing new chapters, but rather a new book.

The days of the saviour have come and gone.

We must now look *within* to find the hero of humanity.

SECTION ONE

YOUR JOURNEY BACK TO SELF

CHAPTER ONE

YOUR JOURNEY OF REMEMBRANCE

*D*ear Beloved Traveler,

Welcome to your journey of remembrance.

May these reminders evoke within you a deep reverence for the gift of who you are, and an embodied knowing of your DNA : Divine Nature Always.

This is a grand invitation to revel in the magnitude and magnificence of who you *truly* are, and an opportunity to liberate yourself from the mental shackles of material preoccupation and the costly external orientation of your worth and value.

Be kind to yourself as you embark on this journey. Everything has unfolded perfectly.

Things are not falling apart, they are falling together.

Everything is not falling to pieces, it is falling into peace.

If you feel that the fabric of your existence has been ripped apart, please remember you *are* the golden thread within all of existence, with a divine seamstress that has woven all.

Any perceived rip in the fabric of your life is sewn by the golden thread of your soul's agenda to bring to light the truth of who you are.

Everything has been infinitely orchestrated for the grand reveal of the power and potency of your majestic eternal being.

Within you, on a 'soulular' level, is a golden thread of eternal knowing.

All that has unfolded is inDEED a part of your Great Awakening, an intimate evolutionary journey of your expansive Self.

Although your ego and personality would suggest that you have lost your way, inherently you have not, nor could you.

> *Your challenges, trials and tribulations are initiations and gatekeepers. They are intentional instigators and catalysts, summoning you to the recollection of who you innately are - Source, Spirit, Creator, God and Infinite Intelligence.*

You are *love* incarnate. It is flowing through you, *as you.*

You are loved and supported beyond measure by the divine intelligence that is within each breath that is gifted to you.

There is nothing you have ever done or could ever do that could diminish your worth and value in this world, or keep you from being loved.

Your worth is not quantifiable. It simply *is*, because you exist.

Your heart is the first organ formed in your body and serves as a reminder of the origin of your essential identity and vitality, and the proper order of how to greet yourself.

You have been bestowed with the Ultimate gift. The gift of free will and a beating heart, which will empower reflections in this magnetic paradise in which you live.

Your personal empowerment and awakening to the truth of who you are, creates a massive R.O.I. - a ripple of impact and return on intention.

This R.O.I. automagically benefits all beings across all time and space, and the generations to come, as all is connected through energy and vibration.

As a divine alchemist, you have been graced with the ability to transmute the energies of darkness, despair and challenges into your gifts and unique expression, affording the experience of love on this planet.

Just as the lotus is able to utilize the murky waters to fertilize its symbolic blossom, so can you. Peacocks derive their beauty from eating toxic plants and transmuting these toxins into the vibrant colors of their plumes.

These are both living examples of your innate ability to catalyze your suffering into strength and beauty.

Your opportunity as an alchemist is to transmute the 'toxic' thoughts and murky waters in your life, to derive the steadfast awareness of your essential power and authentic Self.

As a divine alchemist, remember and revere your ability to interpret what has occurred in your journey through the lens of love, and in so doing turn your 'mess' into a 'message' and chaos into brilliance.

> *Your challenges become the bloom of your fragrant existence, and toxic perceptions transmute into authentic expression and radiant beauty. Choosing to become an awakened alchemist in your life affords you the vital experience you were destined to receive.*

The greatest fragrance designers in the world can not compete with the essential notes of *you*. There is no one like you, never has been and never will be. You are a unique emanation of the life force—with God, Source and Spirit the Ultimate designer.

You will never be replicated again. The alchemical blend of your mind, body and soul are all an incredible gift. The syllable of your soul in the conversation of the Universe will echo throughout eternity.

You are being invited to awaken from the illusion of your disconnection to your divinity, and to sober from the hallucination that you are powerless to create your heart's desires and to realize heaven on Earth.

Thank you for choosing to be awake and aware, and for claiming the truth of who you are at such a pivotal time in our human evolution.

It is time to pray and pay reverence to the Source that resides within you, so that all Heaven can break loose.

CHAPTER TWO

THE GIFT OF MY PARENTS SUICIDE

*M*y parents met at a very young age and got pregnant with me unexpectedly. My mother was on the birth control pill when I was conceived. I was born against all odds and attribute this to my undying commitment to being on the planet at this time.

On my parent's wedding day, a day that is traditionally filled with celebration, best-case scenarios, and love based promises, my parents were imagining the worst-case scenario and chose to divorce themselves from their own hearts.

Extremely poor, they created a survival strategy to assure that they could afford to take care of an unexpected me and made a morbid vow that if they ever got caught, they would end their lives.

30 years later my parents fulfilled that vow. Laying down next to each other in a tent in the wilderness, the first signs of winter had dusted the ground and there was a definite chill in the air. As my parents crawled into their tent, they were not alone.

They had with them all of the necessary ingredients for a recipe of everlasting sleep: mental anguish and despair over money, an impenetrable will and emotional bond, a bottle of Vodka and sleeping pills, a CD player and a Celtic CD, a Dr. Kevorkian book on How To Die, a threatening note to anyone who attempted to resuscitate them and a goodbye letter to me.

Nine months later, their bodies were found. They were in their favorite cuddle position, my father on his back, my mother curled up on his left side. I suspect they both checked out long before their bodies did, unable to stay connected within such a fatal choice.

I cannot begin to imagine what they must have gone through knowing this would be the last time they would be in each other's arms and alive in their bodies.

With my mother's head on my father's chest, I can feel so deeply, how she must have felt, realizing the finality of their choice, when she listened to my father's heart... beat slowly to silence.

I would imagine that many may consider a tribute to suicide to be crazy. For the thought of gratitude, amidst the sorrow that can be related with suicide is, in the truest sense of the word, unreasonable.

> *I am not here to "reason", but rather offer my transparency and my unwavering knowing that all that has come to pass, has happened for me. Although I have had my share of sorrow, despair, regret and suffering, I can see the gift in it all now.*

Despite past remnants of my delusional ego that have wanted to scream otherwise, I now see the divinity within all that has unfolded.

I 'real eyes' my cocoon of circumstances were intended for me to become a butterfly and to transform my relationship with life.

My parents choice to end their life, ultimately birthed my new relationship to life and liberated me from the illusion and costly entrapment that my security and freedom resided in the external world.

With all things being connected, my story and my parents story, becomes your story and our collective story. It is intended as a "wake up" call, an "alarm clock" that we can no longer hit snooze on.

All perfectly timed for you to read, as you continue to awaken and return back home to Self.

My journey becomes an instigator for awareness, transformative realizations and ultimate flight, and a potent reflection of our collective cocoon of circumstances that is seeking to transform us into butterflies. All intended to guide us to live lives of true freedom and well-being.

Within these realizations lives authentic gratitude for all that has occurred in my life.

My parents suicide and my brush with suicide after losing millions in the tech collapse, is the ultimate zeitgeist of our times with so many millions facing an existential crisis of unparalleled numbers.

I am humbled to be honoring my parents with this book, and in so many ways they are co-authoring it with me.

It is in reverence to them and my own journey, that I am in devotion to support each of you to awaken at this time - reminding you of the true source of your security and freedom, and the infinite soul's worth of your eternal being.

> *It is through my experiences, exactly how they have unfolded, that I have been given my journey back to Self, and am honored to reflect this wisdom back to you.*

My parents are continuing to fulfill their role in catalyzing a profound shift of the remembrance of our true value and Self worth beyond our net worth.

It is when we have awakened to our innate and magnificent identity that we are in reverence to those that have come before.

It takes three to have a child. My parents "ushered" me here, along with my free will and soul contract. Behind the scenes, there was a Universal play and a Divine Drama with "characters" that were perfectly cast to fulfill their roles, of which my parents are worthy of an "Academy Award" for their performances.

The alchemical blend of my parents' choices were the perfect recipe for my awakening and for my service to the collective awakening at this pivotal time in our human evolution.

From this awareness, I am able to understand and fulfill my soul's purpose through the only variable that is me. It is no accident that I wrote this book at the same age my parents were when they chose to end their lives.

All that I have experienced has been orchestrated by the Divine Conspiracy, of which I am an accomplice, intended to promote the remembrance of my true essence and value, and to facilitate this awareness and remembrance in you as well.

You too are an accomplice in this Divine Conspiracy—for your eyes have graced these words, intimately bound by the fabric of our co-creative web.

CHAPTER THREE

HOW LOSING EVERYTHING MADE ME RICHER

I remember, as if it was yesterday, where I was in my life....

My parents had just ended their lives, due to money stress. In my own form of rebellion and state of grief, I started to fill the void I was feeling with work and making money.

And more work and more money.

And more work. So I could make more money!

I believed that somehow, making more money would appease my sadness. That it would make my pain go away and my fundamental state of insecurity and fear.

I started spending all of my time in my office, watching ticker symbols.

My life was all about productivity and making the next buck. As the stock prices and my accounts went up so did my stress and anxiety levels, mixed with levels of manic elation.

I was completely stressed and this worry took up the majority of my day.

The anxiety became so intense that I remember a few times literally banging my head against the wall and wanting to pull my hair out.

I was on my way to being the richest woman in the cemetery.

The most ironic part of all this, is that I had inherited my parents' estate and came into enough money that I could have 'retired' off of that.

That should have been enough....

Yet I chose to trade in the stock market (as my father had done)—and became caught up in mindless and heartless investments.

There was an energetic umbilical cord that was still attached to my father, and his choices, his form of success, and I'm sure a huge unconscious part of me that still wanted to make my dad proud.

My stress over money soon turned into an obsession with making money, which turned into more stress and the need to make *more* money.

Which created more of an obsession to make more money.

I stopped spending time with my friends and lost touch with the people I loved. I became isolated and spent most of my time in my office alone.

I soon began to see that even with all of this money, I *still* wasn't happy and was anything but secure.

The irony of it all.

I was basing my happiness and security on something external. On a fundamental lie. The lie was that there was such a thing as 'financial freedom'.

I had bought into the cultural hallucination that having money would somehow give me a sense of freedom, security and fulfillment.

What's even more insane, is that I had grown up in an environment where my dad had lectured about Financial Freedom, for as long as I can remember.

He was in pursuit of the elusive "it" his entire life, and even after he accumulated millions, he was never truly free.

This mental prison of anguish and insecurity eventually led to my father's emotional demise and suicide. And yet, I was heading down the same path of self destruction.

I became afflicted with the "If/Then – When/Then" Syndrome....

If I could just make X amount of dollars, *Then* I would be secure. *When* I met my next goal, *then* I would be free to do more of what I wanted. *If* the stock market produced the return on investment that I wanted, *then* I would be happy.

I was so focused on making a buck, but I was killing myself. I was definitely up against 'wall street'.

Ben Franklin once said – "Most people die when they're 25, but aren't buried until they're 75." I was definitely dead inside, going through the motions, waiting to be buried. I had soul'd out.

And then, the unthinkable occurred. I was faced with the tech collapse and lost everything.

Eventually I lost it all. I was completely devastated.

I didn't know what to do.

I felt completely hopeless.

In the blink of a few ticker symbols, I had lost everything.

I was penniless and pointless, feeling worthless and lying in bed all day. Not eating. Deeply depressed. Isolated and in a prison of my own angst.

Soon, my home was in foreclosure and I found myself in an abusive relationship. Everything in my world was crumbling around me.

I decided I just couldn't go on....

I had lost my will to live and decided I was going to end my life.

But instead...*I decided to be vulnerable.*

I reached out to a close friend, and shared with her what I was feeling.

I was so humiliated and embarrassed but I managed to gather some courage and open up to her. I let it all out.

The choice to be vulnerable initiated one of the most life changing experiences of my journey.

My friend looked at me with compassion and understanding. She looked beyond my words, beyond my fear and despair, to the truth of who I was.

Is very difficult to put into words the effect that this exchange had on me, so I'll just say this….

I felt seen for the first time in my life and with that, emerged a pin prick of hope in my heart.

I went and sat down on my couch, and in front of me was a book I had never seen on Chinese Numerology (divinely placed perhaps?:))I was compelled to open the book, and I discovered that there are 9 distinct paths, each with their own theme.

I am a Life Path of a 9. Within the first paragraph it summarized everything that had just happened to me in detail! "You may lose loved ones, you might lose money in the stock market, you might be facing a natural disaster……., but if you can learn to surrender and let go, you will have the most incredible life filled with abundance, adventure and purpose beyond your wildest imagination."

That was my 'ah ha', my 'awakening' if you will, where I sensed that there was a Divine Conspiracy. I had a gut feeling that everything had been orchestrated by a universal benefactor.

In those moments, I started to glean that I was more than just a human being and there was a purpose to my pain. I had no inkling what the purpose was, it was just a deeper sense. Something that I felt on a soulular level and for the first time in my life, I caught a glimpse of a bigger picture.

I had hope for the first time in a very long time. I sensed that I did need to die, but I needed to leave my body out of it. What needed to perish were the costly, delusional ways in which I was relating to myself and to life.

For the next 3 years, I was devoted to the path of "surrender" and "letting go". I was so upstream in my own current of well being, I didn't even know what I was surrendering to, or what I was letting go of.

I spent a lot of time in nature - the ultimate creative force, and was reminded of the pace of grace. I received a lot of downloads and transmissions about the fundamental truth of the state of plentitude and abundance that innately exists and is our birthright.

... I let go of the illusions I had been holding around my worth and value.

...I let go of the costly false beliefs that had kept me trapped in limitation and hypnotized by the notion that my power, security and happiness existed outside of me.

I started focusing on what was meaningful to me. Because I chose to live, I was going to make it matter.

I managed to find a way home again, back to mySelf.

...More than anything else, I remembered that there is nothing more valuable to me than how I feel.

I started to value myself more and more and chose to govern my choices on how I felt, which was a foreign language to me at the time.

I began to renegotiate my own terms, and discovered the Natural Laws that were governing my personal reality.

I realized that if things weren't adding up I could create a new equation.

One of the most profound Laws—The Law of Response—reminded me that MY thoughts are creating MY reality! In this empowering discovery, I began going into my mental fitness gym and did "reps" everyday of deliberately choosing thoughts of gratitude and appreciation.

I soon began to see evidence in the form of opportunities coming my way and with this, I remembered that with all things being energy, I too am energy and govern and shape my reality through the focus of my attention.

I learned to be in harmony with the Laws that are operating behind the scenes. This changed EVERYTHING!! The better I felt, the better it got. The better it got, the better I felt, and when I started to make a direct correlation between my beliefs and what was outpicturing in my life the state of empowerment began.

I began to live in harmony, instead of reaction and opposition, which allowed me to have an experience of true freedom, fulfillment and EASE (which is something I had NEVER experienced before!)

And now, I experience life in a radically different way...

...My anxiety has been replaced by a true feeling of flow and trust that things are happening FOR me, not TO me. *Trust* became my benefactor.

...Instead of feeling afraid that things are falling apart, I have an unwavering sense of security because of my connection to my own power. I know that things are actually falling together" and are unfolding on my bewhole— provided I choose to view it in this way.

I am now living a life of true wealth and I have a deep irrevocable sense of inner peace. I have a life that is both emotionally rich and materially abundant.

I realize now that the point of me losing everything in the Tech Collapse, was not a "loss" at all, but rather a profound GIFT containing the greatest riches I could have imagined.

No amount of money could replace my discovery of the infinite treasure that exists within me, which I could only have realized through those trials and tribulations.

My former life was no life at all. I was a prisoner to money and the mental shackles of my material preoccupation. Fill-fullment should never be confused with Fulfillment.

Every experience of pain, struggle and "loss" was really a "gift in disguise" to help me realize my Self worth beyond my net worth and my innate value.

Each of my experiences afforded me with the character, strengths, and unique gifts I have today, and have enriched me with a life of authentic abundance.

I am a work in progress and celebrate my continued expansion and evolution. I am so honored to be sharing this journey of remembrance with each of you.

My tragedy ultimately became a triumph. My pain lent itself to my purpose.

My suffering was a pathway to knowing my significance, my mess transformed into a message.

CHAPTER FOUR

THE PURPOSE OF YOUR PAIN

*S*uffering is a signpost of your mind's incongruence with your essential Self and misalignment with the infinite potential of your eternal being. When you are misaligned with the magnificent truth of who you are, you will begin to feel this through your emotional guidance system.

You will also suffer if you are attached to the fleeting and impermanent aspects of the material realm.

This internal barometer is intimately connected to the divine love that is coursing through your life. The Universe speaks in varying decibel levels. These decibel levels will get progressively louder until you can no longer hit 'snooze' on your personal wake up call.

At first your soul will whisper to you, and will eventually increase its presence until you have course corrected, become Self-centered and surrendered to life's intention for your Ultimate flow state.

> *All is intended as a divine escort to allow you to live in harmony with your true nature in reaching an Ultimate state of surrender, and to feel the bliss and exhilaration of your life being informed by your true identity.*

From the depths of your despair you can redeem the most potent recognition of your soul. The deeper your pain and suffering is, the greater your opportunity to forge an allegiance with your true Self. The brightest lights have persevered through the darkest nights.

Your decision to participate in this human experience as a soul and as Spirit incarnate was a conscious one, allowing you to revel in your infinite power, guided by love and trust. All born from the contrast of forgetting who you really are.

You are invited to co-create Heaven on Earth with the energy that is breathing you and loving you, fully and completely. There is a "golden umbilical cord" that is championing for you to be fully expressed and to sing your soul song in the orchestra of this existence.

Your challenges become catalysts and ultimately you can realize that there is no such thing as a challenge but rather everything becomes an opportunity to attune your awareness and your perception to the essential truth of who you are - God and Source incarnate and a magnificent creator.

Any up-sets are setting-you-up to live in greater congruence and confluence with the divine benefactor of your life, which will pay out dividends of abundance and wellbeing always and in all ways.

If you feel you are 'losing it', this is an indicator that you are being guided on the path to finding greater coherence with your essential Self. The longer you turn in opposition to life's beneficial current, the more overwhelmed and discouraged you will feel.

The deeper your pain and suffering the more opportunity you have to truly unite with your essence. Embracing your challenges and experiences as spiritual gifts and initiations is so vital for sustainable states of greater well being, brought forth from this Higher perspective and understanding.

The more your mind defies your infinite power and true Self, buys into a mistaken identity, and/or attaches to the external, the more despair you will feel. This is your INdicator that you are in contradiction to the essence of life, your true identity, and the innate current and nature of your well being.

You are more than just a human being. The experiences that have been most riveting to you, are ultimately opportunities for you to live a more fulfilling experience and share your gifts with others. Your suffering illuminates where you have abandoned yourSelf.

Your trials and tribulations are instrumental in the symphony of your soul song to create the unique and beautiful character that you are. Your hardships are archeological opportunities that encourage you to excavate yourself within the crevasses of despair and disillusionment to become intimate with your own ancient presence.

In the times that you may feel you have 'lost it', you are beginning to truly find yourSelf. Innate wisdom encourages you to endorse your pain and suffering as something that has happened *for* you, not *to* you.

Depression reveals your incongruence with your divinity and infinite power and illuminates if you have bought into the costly illusion of your powerlessness to create your heart's desires and to receive your birthright of a life that is deeply fulfilling to you.

The more incongruent you are with your essential identity, the more you will suffer. The more you oppose life's bounty of abundance, with your limiting beliefs, and defy your birthright of well being, the more depressed you will become. Suppressing your true Self will lead to suffering. Suppression will cause depression.

Desiring fulfillment from an unreliable source will also create pain and drama, for as long as you tether your emotional wellbeing to the external world you will never be free. There is no need to seek approval or love as doing so will set up states of codependency. In the quiet reserve of your own sovereignty you are held by the divine.

Another cause of pain and suffering is subscribing to the illusion of your powerlessness to create your heart's desires.

The more you negate your heart's desires and disguise your essential identity, the more you will experience dis-ease. The more dis-ease you experience emotionally, the more that will evidence itself in your physical body. Your body is the physical manifestation of your predominant emotional and vibrational state.

Continued states of dis-ease will eventually out picture and evidence themselves in your physical body and change your body's chemistry, including the balance and harmony in your mind.

Choosing to reinterpret your pain and suffering, as something that has happened for you becomes an essential catalyst for you to step fully into your power as a divine alchemist.

Your challenges become sign posts illuminating your path to greater self love, empowerment and sovereignty. When you embrace all that occurs as an essential ingredient in your soul's elixir, the recipe of remembering that all is Holy and Divine, allows for inner peace to take root in your experience.

This includes all of the things you believe have happened *to* you. The painful times you have experienced are gatekeepers for your empowerment. They are instruments that are essential to your Soul song and are the tuning forks for your inner symphony.

As the luminary and loveolutionary that you are, these experiences are the seeds for your soul's mission. Your acknowledgment of 'their' benevolent intent germinates the ultimate fruits of these experiences into a rich harvest and are gateways into the deeper embodiment of your true nature and innate power.

When you are able to release yourself from victim consciousness and the illusion of separation, your life will begin to blossom in fragrant ways. Your new found relationship with challenges and shifting your hardships into heartships is vital to your empowerment and sovereignty.

In the elite classroom of your life, you can choose to treat everyone as a divine teacher and an instrument and tuning fork for you to come into greater congruence with your true Self.

Everyone becomes a mirror for you, reflecting opportunities for you to step into greater love and compassion for yourSelf and therefore others.

We are each escorting each other back home to Self, to unify with the love of who we innately are. Everyone becomes your soulmate, allowing you to mate with your own soul.

If you are going through "it" right now, you have a profound invitation to begin to liberate yourself by asking some simple yet profound questions.

The power that exists within you is so much greater than what you are facing externally and circumstantially.

This inSpirited inquiry and quest-ions initiates a shift in perspective which will allow you to forge an allegiance with your essential Self and peer into your soul's vantage regarding the divine purpose of your pain.

- *What is the divine gift in this experience?*

- *How would I feel if I fully trusted that everything that has unfolded had a benevolent intent and purpose?*

- *What if everything I interpreted as wrong or a mistake, was authored by a sacred author with a divine script line to initiate my hero/heroine's journey?*

Be present within this observation -*who is really suffering?*

Within your compassionate observation you become liberated, for it is your soul identity that is illuminating this awareness. As you recognize that it is your personality that feels victimized, not your soul, you are able to uncover and recover the truth of who you are.

Your stance of elevated understanding and inquiry, will afford you a journey of greater emotional equanimity. Embrace your challenges as 'growth edges' and catalysts for you to embody the realization of your eternal magnificence.

Be aware of the place where you are brought to tears. This is where your greatest treasure resides.

CHAPTER FIVE

SOUL CONTRACT

*W*hen you author your life from the understanding that you have signed a Soul Contract and not forged your signature, this provides a vital foundation of perspective and understanding as you continue your journey in the elite classroom of your life.

This classroom is not based on pass/fail, but rather on benchmarks or gateways into greater states of awareness and Self mastery, ultimately leading you to the liberation of oneness.

During this time of Great Change, you are being given the choice to utilize your suffering as sandpaper for your awakening, and to step into greater states of empowerment, sovereignty and love.

As you continue your journey of awakening and embodiment of your innate Self, you can begin to embrace the real-eyes-ation that your trials and tribulations become sacred catalysts.

Your despair becomes a divine promoter for your greater acknowledgement and reverence for how infinitely powerful you are and is a potent initiation and elixir for embracing the truth of who you are - Source incarnate, with the infinite core of an eternal being.

> *The greatest opportunity inherent in your human journey is to awaken to the illusion that you are separate from Source. It is time to mend the costly notion that you are defined by your material reality and your worth is quantifiable.*

Your Earth paced journey is intended for you to resolve the hallucination that you are separate from the Divine love and steadfast support that permeates all of life.

The essential abundance that courses through life itself is yearning for you to recognize the inherent spark of your own magnificence and to align with Its flow.

You are invited within a cosmic embrace, to articulate the essence of the creative source, through the unique variable that is you. The implication of you on life itself is beyond your knowing and beyond measure.

You are a unique and exquisite representation and manifestation of the Divine mind and Infinite intelligence. When you 'real eyes' you are Infinite and that the Divine is flowing through you, *as you*, you are able to claim your power fully and empower yourSelf to wholeness.

Any perceived rip in the fabric of your life is sewn by the golden thread of your Soul's agenda to bring to light the truth of who you are. Cracks and fissures always afford more light, and your human journey is no different.

Catalyzed through the illusion of separation, your hardships become "heartships", and are the cosmic imprints of your Soul's intention to recognize Itself within you. Your trials and tribulations are each curated for the purpose of your expansion and evolution.

It is as though you have to forget in order to remember what you remember, through the contrasting experience of your soul's journey in human form.

Your breakdowns cultivate breakthrough opportunities to have your heart broken open, in order to unite with the infinite perfection of your soul's journey.

Your soul is beckoning you to be reminded of your Self worth and intrinsic value and to live the life you have innately endorsed.

You have been given VIP access to an incredible and rare opportunity to experience life from the earthly plane. A chosen one inDEED with a waiting list to incarnate here.

The syllable of your soul is a vital element of the poetic Universal conversation. The Divine blueprint of your soul contract will always pronounce itself in the perfect way to capture your attention.

These energetic clues are how Source will choose to share "Itself" through the only variable that is you. It is through experience itself, and brushing up against your own edges, that you become "wise", which is to say you become the embodiment of what you innately know to be true.

It is only when you are troubled enough that you become receptive to the conversation of your soul and your Souls' agenda and purpose in this lifetime.

Coded within you is the very essence of Life itself as demonstrated in the cross section of a DNA strand, which exemplifies the Flower of Life. Within every molecule of your being is a core vibration which exists in the totality of all of life.

On a quantum level, you are pure energy and can never be diminished or destroyed. The ultimate recycling program of changing form. Your very nature IS the essence of life itself.

As you begin to harmonize your attention to this knowing, you begin to raise your frequency in congruence with Infinite Intelligence which governs all of the beautiful chaos of your human journey.

Imagining yourself as a living lotus, your Soul's delight is to grow from the murky waters, into the fragrance of your embodied divinity.

The peacock eats poisonous plants and is able to transmute these toxins into the beautiful plume of it's feathers - one of nature's super models. This can serve as a symbolic reminder of your ability to alchemize any toxicity and challenges in your life into a royal plume of your own magnificence.

In its infancy, a dragonfly feels an impulse to propel itself from within the inner recesses of its own being onto a rock all in divine timing, prompting its transformation into the next evolution of its existence. This Earth-paced migratory pattern unfolds in accordance to its own evolutionary capacities and innate plan.

From this new found existence, it receives the life-giving force of the Sun. This omnipotent life force instigates the manifestation of it's dormant wings, ultimately giving flight to a multidimensional experience - subterranean, amphibious and winged one.

> *You too, have a series of initiations and migrations, governed by a benevolent Infinite Intelligence. These initiations are propelling you through an innate knowledge of a multidimensional experience being played out on the Earth stage.*

Embedded in your life's through lines are activations of a deep memory and knowing within the multiverse of your existence.

When you are able to be *in* the world and not *of* it, you can experience your true nature and magnificence in the context of this magnetic paradise.

Encoded throughout your journey and divine drama, resides an inner script line that plays out within your soul's adventure, activating a deep memory of your own knowing.

The temple of remembrance exists inside, this is where you are invited to humbly reside within the most revered and sacred site that is you.

Every day you are blessed with the opportunity to disrobe your unworthiness and step into the regality of your divine nature. It is time to dwell in your inner mansion.

The manifestation of your heart's desires are contingent on your awareness of your worthiness and your recognition that you are Spirit and Source incarnate.

When you go within, you never go without.

You have deliberately signed up in this Free Will/ Free Won't agreement field to recognize your essential Self. Your embodiment of this knowing, incites the grand articulation of the love that is here *for* you and *IS* you.

Delight in knowing that you are God/dess and sit upon the inner throne of your royalty. This will provide the tarmac for the future generations to embody the humble privilege of being human.

The only requirement to realizing the heaven on Earth that already exists, is the ownership of your Souls signature, which in turn promotes the authentic, essential, and vital variable that is you.

As you recognize and real-eyes that Infinite intelligence is within you, this affords credibility from within, returning you to the pure essence of being 'IN-credible'.

> *From this energetic galactic stance of inner affluence, your life becomes a wellspring of eternal offerings, as you choose to claim the day to day mecca of revering your divine nature in the ritual of your everyday life.*

Stand on your internal podium and claim your gold medal for showing up- front row to the greatest show on Earth- your Grand awakening.

When the story of your life is read in the akashic library of your soul, all of the words of existence will never encompass the exquisite (w)holy poem that is you.

CHAPTER SIX

YOU ARE NOT ALONE

*T*he Maya of illusion would suggest that what is seen is all that exists, however there is so much more than meets the eye. You are not alone and are supported in the unseen realms beyond the scope of what your linear mind could ever conceive.

During your souljourn on this planet, you are gifted and graced with your own spiritual entourage and benevolent support team that exists beyond the veil. There is so much honor, respect and reverence for your courage in choosing to be here.

> *This multiverse of existence is packed full with a myriad of sponsors and ambassadors of well being, here to promote a life of fulfillment and joy for you, and to whisper sweet "somethings" into your being. What can not be seen, sings within everything that can be seen. You have a direct line into the Divine.*

The experience on our beloved planet operates in a free will paradigm and agreement field which means you are an intimate collaborator. It is essential that your request and support from the spirit realm is welcomed and deliberately invited by you.

You must evoke your desire to be supported, which is being 'heard' through your vibrational asking, steeped in reverence and trust, and amplified through your affirmations.

Asking for help is a strength and offering you support is a deLIGHT to your council and team. You can begin to receive support from your entourage of support by simply stating out loud:

- *I am open to being supported now.*

- *Please guide me to the path of solution.*

- *I am supported always and in all ways.*

- *I trust that I will receive all of the support I need to thrive in my life.*

- *I am loved and worthy of realizing my purpose and thriving in service to my heart.*

Keep in heart, support will come in a myriad of ways, through sponsors and ambassadors of well being, orchestrating serendipitous connections and soulutions on your bewhole.

Each will be imbued with inspiration, encouragement and clarity of when to act and when to rest and restore. All will be offered in an Earth paced manner that will parallel the cadence of the waxing and waning of the moon and the ebb and flow of the tides.

Communications will not be linear, but will come on a quantum intuitive level. As a multidimensional being you will source your way to understanding and interpreting these beneficial messages.

Your life will become a living tarot of symbolism with loving messages and clues encrypted in your day to day journey -*the Ultimate treasure hunt.* Packaging will vary, however the essence will be divine, guiding you to the richness of your fulfillment.

Embrace a state of no-thingness knowing it is the genesis of all creation. There is a sacred entourage at your back, promoting an intimate and irrevocable knowledge of your Self worth and core identity.

Never lose hope dear one, miracles reside in the invisible. You have an auspicious team that is championing your happy new beginning.

CHAPTER SEVEN

HINDSIGHT IS 2020

*C*ORONA-tion: The ceremony of crowning a sovereign.

CRISIS: The turning point of a dis-ease when an important change takes place, indicating either recovery or death.

APOCALYPSE: The lifting of the veil.

The year 2020 propelled the world into an unprecedented existential and economic crisis that will exceed that of the Great Depression.

As the waves of distress continue to have a ripple effect, we can look to the symbology of CORONA and Coronation, as the time of Great Awakening. The Great Awakening intended to crown us with the remembrance of our sovereignty, our essential worth and what we innately value.

As the machine of materialism is on its last cog, it is time to liberate ourselves from an external orientation of our value and worth. A powerful reformation is upon us.

> *We are at a time of quickening catalyzed by the intense suffering due to dysfunctional premises - a costly and false reliance on money for our security, and the external to guide our lives and assign our worthiness.*

We have had a case of 'mistaken identity' for far too long which has manifested as dis-ease and depression. A costly narrative which has promoted a fleeting sense of security and worth, is now being rewritten.

Each of us is being invited to author authentic and fulfilling scripts for ourselves and for our beloved planet, during this time of Great Change. We are being shaken awake, with an alarm clock that we can no longer hit 'snooze on'.

If you are feeling the rug has been pulled out from underneath you, it is time to remember that you are the "rug". You can rest assured that there is light at the end of the tunnel - *for you are the light.*

Mother Nature in Her infinite wisdom will catalyze great change through what the ego would interpret as devastation, however the forest fires of seeming "devastation" actually propagate richer, more fertile soil from which new life will sprout.

> *Your past can become the compost for your richest soul, and the most fertile soil on be-whole of your future, future generations and our New Earth.*

As the old ways dissolve, dismantle and draw their last labored breaths, and with that the dissolution of the known, a grand opportunity is before you to get deeply in touch with the true basis of your flourishing. This connection and remembrance within you is paramount.

As the financial climate continues to intensify, the reorientation and recalibration process has begun, and with that an inherent opportunity to forge and configure a new path of true security, freedom and fulfillment.

Something is emerging that is deeper than anything your mind has perceived. If things don't add up, you have the opportunity to create a new life affirming equation where the sum total benefits all beings.

The gift of the 'grace period' and 'recalibration time' of 2020, offered an opportunity to begin a new trajectory and actualize your souls 'destiny' and a heart core future.

> *You are being graced with intense experiences to define your worth and value from within, liberating yourself from the external orientation and fleeting standards that have held you prisoner in the mental shackles of material preoccupation.*

Through your trials and tribulations you are bestowed with an intimate awareness of your soul's worth, and are granted the opportunity to embody your Self worth beyond your net worth.

Your separate self, which assigns your co-dependence on an outside agency for your well being, is in the process of dying and relinquishing its grip on your experience. A necessary requirement for initiating sustainable vitality and security.

Your ability to be sovereign and derive your wellbeing and security from within, is of paramount importance at this time.This is a graduation ceremony for You old soul, for the seismic occurrences that are happening in your ENvironment are here to shift your INvironment.

It is essential to perceive that all that has unfolded, has been advocating for you to awaken to your sacred birthright of authentic abundance and to identify with your internal and eternal being. Everything has been falling together in accordance with a divine plan, and life is happening for you.

As you remember your infinite power, you will in-form a new way of relating to your worth and wealth. This will allow you to be immune to victim consciousness and no longer buy into the costly notion that you are powerless and therefore reactive to your circumstances. You will step into steadfast resilience that is only born from within, to become the deliberate co-creator of your own experience.

There is an Ultimate producer that has authored a divine script line, which is being played out to amplify a new template and operating system from which to relate to yourSelf and others, and the Ultimate reflection of our states of consciousness - our beloved planet.

> It is time to pray to your essential magnificence, and in so doing no longer fall prey to the falsities and deceptions of your ego, which would imply that you are limited in your ability to create your hearts desires and that you are separate from the oneness that is inherent in all things.

You have an opportunity to begin anew, no longer writing new chapters in an old story line, but rather a new book with a life enhancing script, utilizing your experiences as a rich compost to propagate your most fulfilling experience yet.

You were born for this pivotal time. This is a time that you have deliberately incarnated for to simply, yet powerfully anchor Love and Light, as we birth the New Age.

It is time to cultivate the consciousness of an awakened soul. Every experience in your life can be utilized as a catalyst to open your heart to your own (w)holy-ness and thereby elevate your states of consciousness and harmony with all of life.

Contained within the courageous acknowledgment of your own despair and powerlessness, resides the union with your core identity. Within your recognition of a disparate existence, you realize there is a compassionate observer that senses there is something more that is available for you.

From this cosmic context and vantage, you are viewing yourself through the lens of your essential Self, eternal Soul and the divine. This grand reveal on a 'soulular' level is opening the can of butterflies for your metamorphosis, witnessing your eternal hero/heroine's journey.

When you enter deeply into a relationship and devotion to this process, you are in courtship with grace herself. To accept this divine invitation is to truly know yourself, and with that dissolve and dispel the fractal notions of separation, catalyzing a higher receptivity and embodiment of your majestic core.

It is time now for your true Universal and eternal nature to be revealed, known and felt by you. You are being invited to learn how to be the captain of your ship and your own LightHouse – no longer being lost in an ocean of despair.

Dive into an ocean of Self devotion and reverence for your eternal journey and allow for a hearty Self centeredness – allowing yourself to be centered within yourSelf and INcredible in the truest sense of the word.

The Old must be released so the New can be realized. When we accept a Universal order and are able to perceive beyond the physical, we can begin to recognize that the ego's interpretation of chaos is vastly mistaken and costly to our levels of trust.From this Higher perspective you can see that all renovation projects involve demolition, and the architecture of our new Earth is no exception.

As a collective we are on the precipice of becoming a graduate civilization that does not destroy itself, but rather reveres the reflection of the divine in all beings and in the planet. Setting us on the course of an altruistic and deeply fulfilling future.

We are in the process of resolving the ultimate zeitgeist of our time and exposing the false concepts and beliefs that have kept us trapped in limitation and hypnotized by the belief that our source is outside of us.

> *You are on a path back home to yourSelf, a path back to your true value, your true abundance, and the power to manifest your purpose and potential beyond what you have imagined possible.*

It is time to realize your inner empire and build your Inner Wealth Portfolio, as you architect an experience that is based in love and trust. You are being initiated into a vital paradigm shift and reformed mind set regarding your fundamentally flawed relationship with money and your current value system.

A refreshing precedent for a new standard of success is being initiated, courtesy of the trials and tribulations that you have experienced. This new precedent for success is founded upon the most valuable aspect of your experience which is based on how you feel.

It is time to dispel the illusion of financial freedom, and real eyes why this pursuit is both fleeting and false, and is the impetus for the majority of the suffering that exists in our world, personally as well as collectively.

When you remember that you are creating from the inside out, you see that true freedom, success, and prosperity is an inside job/joy. When you go within, you never go without.

If you are fearful of the unknown, it is vital to remember that you are crafting your destiny through your choices in any given moment. The choice of fear or love. Doubt or trust. Your future is in its formative stage now. And now. And now.

You have the ability to co-create Heaven on Earth. You were born for this time. As a vibrational human being you are creating your experiences in every given moment.

Your most potent choice resides in the placement of your attention and the stories that you tell. Everything in your life is based on a story, the most important story being the one you tell yourself.

What story will you choose to tell about the year 2020?

Will you regurgitate the same stories over and over and ensure that His/ Herstory repeats itself?

Or are you ready to author a new script, using the ink of your own divinity, written on the scrolls of your eternal knowing?

> *The frequency you broadcast is returned to you always and in all ways. Where you place your attention is where you will dwell. You can create Heaven or you can create Hell.*

If you realize that things are not adding up for you and the planet, it is time to create a new heart core equation. The best way to predict your future is to create it.

One of the most potent invitations is to surrender to the Unknown, the birthplace of all creation. The template of existence on this planet is intended for you to have an experience of empowerment, love, truth, compassion and thriving as you share your gifts with others.

The co-creation of a world that works for everyone and the manifestation of Heaven on Earth, is seeded in your recognition of how divine and worthy you are, to be here now.

You have an opportunity now to create a version of reality that is far more resonant and authentic than the one you were previously living. It is time to open the flood gates of your eternal worth. This is the essence of Free Will or Free Won't.

Let wellbeing flow into your life, forever funded by the ultimate resource of Source, with trust being your ultimate benefactor.

You are an essential and vital vibrational midwife in the birth of our new paradigm. Your elevated states of consciousness can be born out of your suffering and despair - if you so choose.

The choice is before you to revere your challenges and tribulations as catalysts for your divine remembrance. Will you allow these traumas and dramas to fulfill their sacred role - to inform your greater awareness of Self and conscious choice?

Will you allow them to be the instrumental catalysts for your soul song, and intentional keys to liberate you from mental slavery and the anguish of an external orientation - graduating you into a grand new experience?

During this time of Great Decision your choice is the essence of Free Will and Free Won't and is in-forming what will manifest.

The universal embryo is within you now and grants you the opportunity to birth anything. You are "pregnant" with infinite potential.

CHAPTER EIGHT

REDEFINING SUCCESS

*T*rue success is founded on emotional well being. Your emotional well being is directly correlated to your inner dialogue, the stories you tell yourself and the focus of your attention. Is there anything more valuable to you than how you feel?Experiencing greater fulfillment begins with nurturing your core relationship with yourSelf.

Often when people are focused on self care, they are focused on secondary nutrition - diet, exercise, body treatments, etc. Although this intention is wonderful, the origin of your reality and your results (including your health) is based on your thoughts and states of consciousness.

> *This is the essence of primary nutrition. Life treats you the way you treat you. Every relationship in your life is a reflection of the relationship you have with yourSelf.*

The following "5 P's" are key ingredients in the recipe of emotional well being. They will assist you with a healthy relationship with yourSelf and to meet all that is unfolding in your journey with grace and compassion.

Progress, Process, Patience, Perspective, Practice

#1: *Honor your progress.*

Instead of focusing on all of the things you have yet to accomplish (with a To- Do List that perhaps extends beyond your life span), or being fixated on the ways you think you need to improve yourself, take time to celebrate your progress. Take stock in your magnificence and evolution.

What you focus on expands, so the more you honor your progress, the more you will progress. Most importantly, the more you celebrate what is right about you, how courageous you are and all that you have gleaned throughout your journey, the better you will feel about yourself.

#2. *Realize that your life is a process.*

Acknowledge that each trial and tribulation and perceived 'setback' is an opportunity to catalyze your experiences for the purpose of greater clarity and fulfillment. The process known as 'life experience' is something to embrace.

Each experience provides a building block of greater awareness and with that an opportunity for making a wiser choice next time. It is a process, as each experience you have had is promoting who you have become.

#3. *Offer patience to yourself.*

Patience is indeed a virtue. Why? It feels better to be patient with yourself and to trust the timing of what is unfolding. The cosmic irony is the more patient you are in your life, the more things will flow in your favor.

One of the primary ingredients in being able to be patient, has to do with your ability to trust in the intelligence that is coursing through all of life. This infinite intelligence has the capacity to coordinate timing in a way that your ego mind can not possibly comprehend. What is the hurry anyway?

It is not about the manifestation of the 'thing' it is about your creative journey along the way. As an infinite creator you will never ever be complete, so take yourself out of the pressure cooker and enjoy your experience.

The 'whole of existence' knows to trust the process and to be patient. We can see the innate levels of trust in the greatest creative force of Mother Nature. We can sense that the trees know when to bring flowers, and when to let go and stand naked against the sky. They are just as beautiful in their nakedness, waiting for the new leaves with great trust, releasing the old and allowing the new to come, in Its own timing.

It is in the silence and in the waiting and in the vibration of patience, that you will grow your authentic Self. Within this state of divine dormancy, you are in ceremony with the sacred seasons of your life and can produce your richest harvest.

#4. _Operate from a higher perspective._

How you perceive yourself, your life and what is unfolding, is the most vital informant of your emotional well being. When you choose to operate from a higher perspective or eagle eye perspective, you are able to liberate yourself from drama.

Choosing to perceive your challenges through the lens of "how is this happening for you" and how are things falling together, instead of "apart", allows you to step into greater self mastery and become a sacred alchemist in your life.

Looking at your journey from a cosmic perspective affords a grand acknowledgement of how intimately orchestrated your Soul's journey has been, and will continue to be. Remember we can not always see the 'forest amidst the trees'.

Allow yourself the retrospective that time will afford you, and choose to investigate how Spirit was championing for the best possible outcome for your evolution and fulfillment.

#5. _Realizing your life is a practice._

It is nourishing to remember that you are learning through contrast - the Ultimate stimulus package, or what some refer to as 'mis-takes'. As you real -eyes there is no such thing as a wrong note in the symphony of your existence, you can embrace these experiences with their divine purpose in mind.

Just as you can choose to sample a variety of flavors of ice cream to decide what you like most, life is dishing up a variety of flavors for you to choose from as well. Embrace these varying experiences as the 'sign posts' to support your direction, conscious choice and union with your essential self.

Each experience you have ushers you to greater clarity. Your clarity is one of your super powers. When you choose to apply your greater awareness to making higher choices you are able to develop your character. The more you practice operating in integrity with your true Self and innate character, the more you will experience personal well being and vitality.

Being consistent with certain life affirming practices on a daily basis will also grant you the ability to be congruent with your true Self. You are being invited to wake up each morning declaring the 5 P's to yourself. This will ensure that you wake up on the "right" side of the bed each day.

Declaration:

Today I choose to honor my progress, offer patience to myself, operate from a Higher Perspective and real-eyes my life is a practice and it is a process.

CHAPTER NINE

SELF WORTH BEYOND NET WORTH

One of the most costly notions "to your well-being" is that your worth, security and fulfillment resided in the external world. You are here to awaken to the Ultimate hallucination within your incarnate journey, that you are separate from the life force itself and that your worth is quantifiable.

If things don't add up, you have the ability to create a new equation. The Old paradigms and ways of relating which have been fundamentally costly to your wellbeing are asking to be revitalized and reconfigured.

If you feel at times like you can't go on and want to end your life, this is an invitation to real eyes that what is wanting to die has nothing to do with your body. Exiting your physical form will not provide 'sustainable' relief as the "Ultimate recycle program" of energy will ensure that your lesson of 'getting it' will continue to perpetuate Itself, until the essence of your true identity is known by you.

The Ultimate death is the one of the ego and the illusion that you are separate from Source and powerless to create your heart's desires. In your recognition of the Divine plot, you can embrace your trials and tribulations as initiations on the path of your realization of your essential identity, and with that true fulfillment.

Once this is realized your life becomes a living tarot, where your states of consciousness and relationship to yourself is mirrored back to you. Your suffering reflects that you have assigned your security, worthiness and freedom to the external.

Depression correlates to a sense of powerlessness in your life with the most rampant misnomer being in your relationship with money and your inability to express and share your gifts in the world and thrive in doing so.

Each trial and tribulation becomes a catalyst for the return of an essential knowing of your intrinsic worth and value. A valuation that is derived from within, and is always paying dividends of bounty and abundance.

Banking on the inherent wealth that is coded in your DNA affords the multitude of affluent reflections in your life, courtesy of the Ultimate resource of Source itself of which you are an intricate part of.

When your ego seeks a quantifiable measurement of your success, you are placed in the mental shackles of material preoccupation. As long as you assign your worth, value and well being to anything external you will never truly be free.

The egoic spreadsheet of right and wrong, and quantification and value based on fleeting standards and accolades have lost their illusive luster and are inviting a deeper internal shine from your Self worth

You are being given the Ultimate reset to be in the world, but not of it – to recognize and illuminate that everything that out-pictures in your reality is but a reflection of the relationship you have with yourSelf. The Universal banking system pays the highest dividends when you humbly own your divinity and the sacred journey of your existence.

During this time of Great Change, you are being invited to illuminate your path of worth and wealth from an intrinsic place. Recognizing and remembering that all form is born from consciousness and from vibration, which is in-formed by your primary beliefs, and your core relationship with yourself.

Everything in your existence is based on a story with the most important story being the one you tell yourself. This awareness automagically dissolves the hallucination of separateness, and forges a path of Divine Union within yourself if you so choose, which will allow you to be IN-credible.

As you step into your cathedral of consciousness, any case of mistaken identity and being on the fast track of being materially rich but emotionally broke is resolved, and the delusional path of fil-fullment instead of ful-fillment is dissolved.

This deep restoration of sovereignty, affords you the opportunity to command the power that is dormant within you to fertilize a rich fulfilling experience of abundance and internal state of affluence.

From your state of remembrance you can fertilize this essential soil through a level of innate empowerment and command creation from a deep knowing and reverence of the gift of who you are.

With a renewed 'inside out' orientation, you can rest assured in the unfolding and the grand plan at play. Trusting and relaxing into the unfolding allows for the richest harvest for yourself and for the planet.

This awareness, awakening and reclaiming of your true nature and core identity, propagates and seeds a new reality from the fertile garden of your consciousness.

This sovereignty allows for the natural emanation of the fragrance of your infinite and eternal being. The foundation of your essential identity and essential Self, illuminates the path of the manifestation of our collective new reality and Heaven on Earth is realized in your alliance with your spirit knowing that it in-forms the material plane.

The Ultimate allegiance with your infinite Self allows for the out-picturing of a world that works for everyone. No longer shackled to an outside- in orientation, but rather in-formed from your core identity. As you align your frequency and your vibration to your essential and innate worth, you real-eyes that everything is generated from the inside out.

This fosters a vibrational tone and harmony with all that Is, allowing for a thriving existence. Liberated from the shackles of material occupation as an indicator of worth and value - you can allow yourself to emanate from a deep seated awareness of your intrinsic value. This is the time for your inner affluence to broadcast your essential worth.

Your priceless nature affords the greatest liberation of all. To know that within your being, resides all that is ever needed, all that ever was and all that will be. When you go within you never go without. You will soon wonder why you ever limited your state of abundance by focusing on your bank account.

Life is a kaleidoscope, with each aspect of your journey becoming a facet of your greater awareness. The infinite cycle of creation that exists within you on a cellular and soulular level catalyzes the most benevolent unfolding.

In-scripted and in-coded within your unfoldment and awakening is the Ultimate production team, offering divine dramas that represent a cast of characters all fulfilling their roles perfectly.

The Ultimate Script - your journey of remembrance, playing out on the Earth stage, the evolution of your union with your true identity. Each dynamic and each scene encoded with a divine blueprint - the evolution of your own realization of your essential self.

On a soulular level, you have been given an opportunity to remember. There is a divine script that has you play out the role of victim only to awaken to the realization that God/ Source is flowing through you as you.

The residency of deep security lies within the recognition of yourSelf and your Soul, which then promotes and illuminates your sense of peace and purpose. Life treats you the way you treat you.

> *The previous, costly co-dependency of relying on external forces to validate you is liberated and dissolved as you step into the awareness that you are a Self fulfilling prophecy.*

When you align your attention to the remembrance that you are co-creating your reality with the energy that is breathing us and 'life-ing' you, you will shift into allowing the energy of goodwill and abundance to permeate your experience.

Trust becomes your ultimate benefactor, affording a deep state of peace and relaxation as you deliberately co-create your reality with the energy that creates worlds and galaxies.

As you attune your awareness to the infiniteness of your own being, and your Soul's worth, this translates to an experience of unwavering trust and empowerment. Operating from this place allows you to collaborate with the divine through your vibration, allowing for the poetic outpicturing of the beauty, love and grace that you are.

Blessed are those that are silent in reverence and humility, knowing that God, Infinite Intelligence and Source is within. It is not separate from you or "out there". As you focus your prayers and intentions on the spirit that dwells within you, *as* you, abundance abounds.

As you breathe in this acknowledgment you will begin to feel the potency of your being and begin to understand just how innately powerful you are to define your reality.

Your worthiness and your value is validated by the creed of your existence. Sit upon the throne of your own divinity. Adorn yourself with the awareness of your magnificent journey. Dine from the banquet of your inner harvest.

Wear the robe of your luminosity on the runway of your life, and in so doing allow the riches to pour forth from the treasure chest that is you, dancing in harmony with your partner in shine - the infinite resource of Source.

This is a prime time to connect with the essence of your eternal identity and open the flood gates to authentic abundance. There is so much more to you than what meets your eye. There is no one like you - never has been and never will be.

You belong here. The Universe knows your name. Honor your path. Celebrate your uniqueness. The implication of YOU on Life itself is beyond your knowing and beyond measure, and will reverberate throughout eternity.

All Heaven will break loose on your be-whole as you rise in love with yourSelf, as the luminous loveolutionary that you innately are. As you connect with the essence of all creation as the core of your identity, you liberate yourSelf to express as the pure creative force that is inherent in your being.

Your embodiment of your soul's worth and Self worth is the new currency from which all abundance will manifest itself, and prosperous soulutions will reveal themselves.

As you employ kindness and compassion for yourSelf and therefore others you will stimulate the economy more powerfully than ever before, allowing the reflection of money to be an appreciation currency reflecting your dharmic value.

CHAPTER TEN

THE DIVINE CONSPIRACY

*W*ith everything being based in energy and vibration, there is an undercurrent of wellbeing and a benefactor that is championing for you to live a life of vitality and authentic abundance.

This benevolent energy is evidenced in the intimate choreography of your physiology and the spinning of the Earth on her axis in perfect proximity to a life-giving Sun. This loving energy goes by many terms - Spirit, God, Source, Infinite Intelligence Universe and Creator - to name a few.

In the moment that you are clear about your heart's desires your only business is to focus on *what* you are wanting and *why* you are wanting it.

Once you are clear with the essence of what you are most wanting, the Divine will conspire to auto*magically* deliver to you all cooperative relationships for your fulfillment, to include *how*, *when*, *where* and with *whom*.

One of the major contributors to a disheartening and overwhelming existence is to use your will power and finite mind to fixate and fret over these details.

This is also one of the main reasons many people have 'To Do' lists that extend beyond their lifetime and heart disease is at an all time high. High degrees of stress are felt in the system based on a delusional attempt at managing these details.

You are being invited to relinquish these details to the same intelligence that is able to digest your last meal and transmute those energies into your life force. The infinite resource of Source has your back, front and all sides.

This omnipotent loving force is 'managing' the infinitesimal details of existence in every nanosecond, and can easily orchestrate the cooperative components needed for your heart's desires to come to fruition. This is all organized by the ultimate creative force of Mother Nature, all in divine timing and in service to the seasons of your evolution.

Given that Spirit and Source are flowing through you as you, you are also a key collaborator and must also partner with this life-giving energy by being in vibrational harmony with these desires.

You harmonize with your heart's desires by focusing on the essence of *what* you are wanting and *why* you are wanting it. *'What'* you are wanting is your clarity, which is an essential seed in the creative process. Your *'why'* will make you cry with tears of joy and deLIGHT - all indicators of your unification with your soul mission in this lifetime and congruence with your birthright of experiencing passion, purpose and prosperity.

Once you feel into the essence of *what* you are wanting and *why* you are wanting it, begin to invoice what is working and what you are grateful for in your life, which will elevate your vibration to be congruent with your desires.

Remembering that your heart is the first organ formed in your body, a heart's desire is anything that is life affirming, life promoting and creates a world that works for everyone.

> *When you stop 'shoulding' on yourself and start honoring your heart-core desires, you will align with your entourage of support to champion the highest and most benevolent outcome for all.*

Knowing that you are attracting based on how you feel, you can rest assured that in a short amount of time you will soon see energetic 'breadcrumbs' of new evidence deLIGHTING the runway of your journey, as the Universe showers you with blessings.

The ingredients of your alignment and Divine Intelligence is a winning recipe for your fulfillment in every way, for not only are your desires realized, you get to enjoy the creative process by being in a state of ease, grace and trust.

When you replace your will power with Divine Will, there will always be a way.

CHAPTER ELEVEN

ANCESTOR TRIBUTE

*S*eeded in the journey of those that have come before, is your dormant divine potential. The Ultimate reverence to your ancestors is in your awakening. As a living ancestor yourself, the journey's of the ancestors that have come before are the divine algorithm inherent in your DNA- Divine Nature Always.

When you choose to awaken to the truth of who you are and honor your core identity of Source and the Divine, you elevate your lineage. Embodying your magnificence pays tribute to the extraordinary journeys that have come before.

Your ancestors' experiences serve as gatekeepers to your greater awareness and coherence with your innate Self. All trials and tribulations are initiations for your spiritual evolution.

These initiations set forth a vibrational landscape that allows you to cultivate a state of peace that allows for the resonance of a higher vibration, born from the knowing that all has been divine.

Breaking through the illusive ceiling by allowing and choosing a life of joy, Self acknowledgement and expression is a vital tribute to your predecessors. When you choose to have your life all of the way, you set a new precedent and energetic tone for future generations to come. Your Self realization becomes encoded in their DNA.

This is the gift that keeps on giving through time immemorial, as the new seeds of humanity reap the energetic seeds of your vibrational harvest. They are the off-spring of your state of well being.

Your life becomes a symbolic skyscraper, each elevated floor built upon the experiences of your predecessors. Your ancestors each dwelled within one of the stories below. Some may have awakened more to the truth of who they were, some a little less, some maybe not at all.

Those that did, would elevate one, two or three stairs, or perhaps one full story in the realization of who they truly are. Each elevated level of awareness was a foundation for your current elevated vantage.

Your perceptiveness and wisdom is granted from the courageous family of souls that have come before. Where you reside, and the perspective you have in the skyscraper known as your life, is due to the journeys of those that have come before.

The symbology of a story in a building is significant as the lives of your ancestors were built upon the stories of who they believed themselves to be, and what was possible for their life.

> *As you choose to consciously witness and acknowledge the poetic orchestration and perfection of all of the previous journeys, you can see that each one was a sacred building block in the crystalline construction of who you have become.*

The vantage that you have now for what you can architect in your life, is made possible by all of the laymen/women that have come before. Their trials and tribulations are all part of a sacred grid, unfolding in accordance to a Higher plan.

If you are in judgment of your ancestors, this creates a costly ripple effect of pain and drama. When you choose to offer compassion and embrace their journeys, this state of deliberate honoring allows you to alchemize any riffs and alkalize your DNA.

This choice allows you to be more present for the gifts that are inherent in your life now, and paves the way for future generations to experience a new energetic template to experience their life from.

The choice to revere the pioneers of your journey, imprints a new energetic template from which our planet and her inhabitants will profit greatly.

Honoring all of the journeys exactly how they have unfolded. Those that awakened to the truth of who they are, and those that did not, are all embraced within the Divine Conspiracy and the Earth paced cadence of evolution.

When you honor the collective journey of your own evolution of awakening, and acknowledge the spirit of Divine order, you can then begin to own more fully, your true nature and innate power.

> *When you choose to revere the many facets, reflections and players in your journey, this fertilizes the path for future generations. Recognizing your familial timeline as champions for your greater states of divine unity, you are able to holistically embody all aspects of yourself.*

Each ancestor compelled and informed an initiatory journey into evolved states of consciousness. Born from the contrasting experiences of despair and powerlessness which were informed from being disconnected to their true nature.

It is within your compassion and reverence for your predecessors, that you become an amplifier and champion for the generations to come to live their fullest potential as Source incarnate.

> *Time is an illusion, frequency is the true clock of existence. There is no past or future but rather a spiral of the ever eternal now, unfolding and expanding simultaneously. You exist on a continuum of energetic pulses that are defined by your states of consciousness.*

Your awakening and the honoring and celebration of those that have come before, is a powerful gift that allows you to transmute your lineage back seven generations.

Recognize the gift that you are giving to yourSelf and to future generations, for within your pure love and acceptance of yourself and your predecessors, you become the fertile soul of your future ancestor.

CHAPTER TWELVE

BEYOND FORGIVENESS

*F*or-giveness is an incredible gift that you bestow upon yourself and others. It is a beneficial choice that is imprinted in the DNA of future generations, and energetically reinforms your ancestral lineage.

There is nothing more depleting to your vitality and self worth than to hold yourself hostage to your past, imprisoned by the notion that you or others have done something wrong.

Believing that others have wronged you, life has harmed you, and things should have unfolded differently, is a very costly illusion and narrative.

'Should-ing' on yourself and others, judging your choices and what has unfolded, is an expensive egoic illusion that discredits the perfect unfoldment of your soul's journey.

The perception of being "off path" is also a diminishing construct of your mind and carries with it insidious layers of judgement and retribution, which in turn hijacks your emotional well being and ability to be present for the gifts of your current life.

Choosing to for-give yourself and others is a potent form of Self love, however 'beyond forgiveness' invites another level of liberation which is derived from your soul's understanding that everything has unfolded according to an Intelligent plan.

When you choose to recognize that everything has unfolded for you and not to you, and that things are falling together and not apart, you begin to realize ("real eyes") there is nothing to forgive.

This benevolent reformation of your past grants you the ultimate honoring of your life experience and becomes a vital catalyst to embody your divinity which in turn affords you a deep state of peace.

Choosing to interpret your experiences from this perspective and posturing yourself on the Earth stage in this way, allows you to reclaim the energy that was previously held hostage in regret.

The word 'sorry' becomes obsolete as you become empowered in the knowledge that each of your experiences were the building blocks of greater awareness and understanding. This affords the ultimate tribute to your human journey ~*wisdom*.

Instead of apologizing and regretting the experiences that fostered your greater awareness, the spiritually accurate reference shifts from being 'sorry' to 'I am now able to make a higher choice."

When you judge your past experiences, you forget that those experiences were the perfect recipe for you to become who you are today, allowing you to gain greater wisdom, empowerment and understanding of your essential self and your in-credibleness.

The irrevocable in-credibility that can only be derived from these experiences is ironically what you signed up for in your journey, with a soul signature that was not forged.

When you go down memory lane and think you should have done something differently, you negate the gift of these expansive experiences.

> *Guilt can never change your past, however residing in compassion and love for yourself, and recognizing a deeper intent to what has unfolded, radically shifts your current emotional experience, and therefore changes the imprint and frequency of your future.*

Your past experiences were sponsored by a divine benefactor to extend to you powerful reflections of your essential power to utilize within your human journey. Each is intended to expand your awareness of your innate abilities and inspire greater compassion for yourself and others, and with that expanded states of consciousness.

These heartcore imprints and discoveries are derived through the elixir of experience. Everything that has unfolded has been the perfect alchemical blend to inspire a deep remembrance within you, and to develop you spiritually and emotionally.

Full acceptance of yourself and others, and the celebration of your journey exactly how it has unfolded, will evoke miracles and magic.

Loving what has transpired will afford the greatest recognition of your authentic Self and journey, and is the purest form of love. Anything other than this is a version of conditional love and places your experience of emotional well being on a contingency plan- always contingent on something needing to be different.

Love is a *given*, despite your ego's notion that it is to be earned, quantified or is conditional. The essence and truth of who you are IS love, therefore you are *always* worthy of it, because you are *it*.

> *On a soulular level and through the eyes of your divine parent, there is nothing you could ever do that could erode your value and worthiness in this life. There is nothing to be for-given, for all is already given.*

Your spiritual entourage applauds your ability to navigate through your human experience with the glow of your heart core identity within your gaze.

Your greater levels of compassion, awareness and intimacy with your true essence, have been garnered from the experiences you have been gifted, especially those that you have deemed the most challenging.

It is within your disappointments that you can choose to appoint yourself with greater awareness and love. Your upsets are intended to set you up for more grace, derived from the acknowledgement of the noble intentions of a divine director.

Divine Will permeates all, and there is nothing stronger and more steadfast than your soul's agenda to recognize *itself* within your being, during your human journey.

Each challenging experience of your past, catalyzes a greater level of understanding and awareness of your power, and the truth of who you are. Your trials and tribulations are the spiritual perpetrator for you to become more intimate with your essential core.

It is within your greatest vulnerabilities that your deepest need arose - the need to merge with the truth of your magnificence.

Every attribute of your journey, produced by a divine benefactor promoting your reverence for yourSelf and your in-credible and courageous choice to be here.

Courage being your ability to tell the story of who you really are, with your whole heart.

Recognize your soul's purpose and rest assured knowing that all has been divinely guided. Bless yourself and others by letting go of guilt and shame. Step onto the inner pulpit of your heart and listen to it's sermon.

This may feel unreasonable and irrational to any parts of you that are relating to aspects of victim consciousness within the human narrative.

You may encounter some "resistance" to this ultimate form of liberation, if you are interpreting your journey through the lens of something other than your Soul's agenda and the Divine Conspiracy.

This is shared with the utmost of tenderness and empathy for those that have experienced the immensity and intensity of painful experiences (myself included).

When you choose to go 'beyond forgiveness' of another, this is not condoning their personal behavior, but is rather a conscious decision to harmonize with a Higher perspective.

Honor and reverence for Self and others is derived from trusting that everything has unfolded in accordance to a higher plan for the evolution and expansion of all, in this lifetime or the next.

When you take things personally and are affected by the actions of another, remember this is your personality being harassed, not your soul.

When you are *not* in a state of trust or acceptance, you are judging. Judgment is a very low vibrational experience, and will continue to dampen the wellbeing that is naturally afforded to you

From a cosmic context, your graduation out of painful experiences and drama occurs when you are able to recognize their benevolent intent, and choose to meet these experiences and yourself with compassion and grace.

In this state of grace and compassion, and ultimately celebration for yourSelf and others, you liberate yourself to be present and to create from a new energetic template.

As you continue your journey of reclaiming and remembering the essence of who you are, you will vividly know that all characters have been deliberately cast in your divine drama. Villains, heroes, accomplices, allies, sacred enemies, all serving as manifestations and reflections of your core relationship with yourSelf.

Suffering exists when you withhold love from yourself and are not trusting in the Divine Plan. Everything and everyone has been cast and designed for your own evolution and remembrance. Each player is a co-creator in the Grand Awakening play.

From your experience of suffering and despair you can catalyze a more embodied recognition of your God Self. When you have amnesia of who you truly are, you will suffer.

Any drama and suffering in your experience is an offering for you to return to greater love and acceptance within yourself. Each experience of powerlessness bestows an opportunity for greater empowerment and in-credibleness.

If you so choose, your suffering can instigate a desire to align more fully with your infinite power and divine grace. The more intimate you become with your sacred journey of intent, the more resourced and resilient you will be.

When you acknowledge the ego's addiction to creating a landscape of perpetual right and wrong and relinquish it's zealous focus on the illusion of separation, you real-eyes that the internal field between right and wrong doing is fostered within the residency of your heart.

When you choose to relinquish the ego's hold of polarity and separation, you surrender into your beingness, and can relax into loving what is, which affords a seismic shift in resonance and frequency.

Beyond forgiveness evokes a great state of Self mastery, which ultimately allows you to shift from judgement to acceptance, and from acceptance to celebration of all of your life experiences.

The experiences you may have interpreted as detrimental to your journey, you now real-eyes were the divine instigators for your reckoning and awakened soul. When you are able to meet your disappointments with grace and compassion, you can transmute the energies that would continue to play out over and over again.

Your journey is deeply seeded in the intention of having you honor, revere and celebrate your divinity through Self love and awareness.

Your past experiences become the enriching compost for your awareness of Self, which in turn fertilizes the harvest of a fruitful present and ripe future.

Each experience a prophet for your soul to profit from it's journey, affording you an evolution into another level of luminosity.

CHAPTER THIRTEEN

PRICELESS RECALIBRATION MANTRA

*T*he Priceless Recalibration Mantra is powerful to utilize if you are experiencing pain and drama in your life. The intention of this practice and this mantra is to inspire you to assume full responsibility for your life through your awareness of your perception and projections. Your perception is creating your emotional experience and therefore reality.

If you are experiencing anything other than love, flow and fulfillment in your experience, this will indicate to you that your perception has been based in lack and scarcity.

As you assume full responsibility for your life through your awareness and conscious choice, you will be empowered to shift any experience of pain and drama into one of love and appreciation.

Acknowledging that when you experience pain and drama in your life, this is representing itself in this way, as a reflection of your perception being based in fear, lack and scarcity.

This serves as an opportunity to clean up your consciousness and to recalibrate to the truth of who you are, which is pure love.

The Priceless Recalibration Mantra is essentially 4 sentences:

I acknowledge, I accept, I appreciate and I love.

Returning to the origin of your experience, which is your perception and your consciousness will allow you to efficiently return to the heart of the matter. This bypasses the expensive indulgence in drama due to perpetual processing and focusing on an outside-in orientation of 'He said, She Said".

Once you are familiar with the core recalibration statements, any time you feel triggered, you may choose to simply state the core mantra – I acknowledge, I accept, I appreciate, I love.

PRICELESS RECALIBRATION MANTRA:

I choose to take full responsibility for my experience.

Anytime I experience pain or drama in my life, it is an opportunity to return to love within myself.

Everything and everyone is an extension of my consciousness and is a reflection of the relationship I have with myself.

I ACKNOWLEDGE

I ACCEPT

I APPRECIATE

I LOVE

I ACKNOWLEDGE that my perception was based in fear and scarcity which manifested as pain and drama.

I ACCEPT myself and all that has unfolded as an opportunity to align more deeply with the truth of who I am, which is pure love.

I APPRECIATE what has been revealed to me and the realizations that have come from this unique experience.

I LOVE myself and trust that life is happening for me. I am *love*.

(Inspired from the ancient Hawaiian mantra of ho'oponopono)

CHAPTER FOURTEEN

WHO DO YOU THINK YOU ARE?

The purpose of your mind is to amplify your divinity. Your mind and heart are partners that support your experience of freedom, fulfillment and prosperity. When the synapses of your mind are attuned to your innate light and true Self, your wattage is amplified. When your mind begins to hijack your intimate knowing of your essential Self, you will suffer.

Your emotions are your heart's intelligence system, which serve as sign posts informing you regarding the direction of your thoughts, indicating whether or not you are aligned with the truth of who you are, and are on your path of Self actualization.

Your internal storyboard paints the picture of what is to come as everything and everyone is a reflection of your inner dialogue. When your mind defies your true Self and you vilify and bully yourself, you deny your magnificence. Never believe a thought that does not empower you.

Be aware of the stories that you tell, you will pay the price in your emotional experience. The divine that is in love with you wants you to love *you* equally, which you do through the stories that you tell yourself.

Looking to the external and to others to define and validate and define who you are is also extremely defeating to your vitality and vibrance. Assigning your sense of identity in this way enables codependency and ultimately resentment towards yourself and others.

With every relationship being a reflection of the core relationship you have with yourSelf, it is important to be INcredible.

The ego mind is also notorious for creating an egoic spreadsheet of checks and balances, garnering payouts based on what you have done, keeping you on the contingency plan of accomplishments for a sense of well being and inner peace. Remember your presence is everything and is enough.

Resolution to an internal power struggle between your ego and your soul resides in your greatest resource which is your focus and your attention. Stepping into conscious awareness of this is key.

What story are you telling yourself now?

- Are you a Naysayer or a Yaysayer for your life?

- Is what you are promoting in your own internal "storyboard" life affirming and feel good?

- *"What are you thinking about now my friend?"* is a love note of awareness and nurturing gesture that can be placed around your home to bring insight to your unconscious inner dialogue.

A Harvard study reported that of the 60,000 thoughts a day on average that are thought, 48,000 of those thoughts were negative for the average American. We are creating based on our thoughts, so shifting this inner ratio is crucial for new opportunities to propagate from the fertile garden of our minds.

It is time to evict the martyr of your mind and overthrow the tyrannical judgemental mind. When the martyr of your mind succumbs to the humility of your souljourn, your magnificence is restored. When your synapses and your soul converge, you embody your authentic power.

Guidance from the Universal mind can be received through meditation, quieting your mind, setting intentions to receive and know your truth and to affirm your magnificence through personal mantras and affirmations.

Focusing on gratitude and all of the things that you appreciate and celebrate about yourSelf will amplify your divinity and your ability to embody your truth in this lifetime. These are all powerful choices to restore within you a strong foundation of direction for your mind to support your journey back to Self. Remember the universe does not profit from you playing small.

CHAPTER FIFTEEN

RADICAL GRATITUDE

*G*ratitude is a perceptual choice to view your life through the lens of love and acknowledging what you are thankful for. This principle is based on your conscious involvement in directing the precious commodity of your attention, in the direction of what you appreciate.

When you look at your life through gratitude and appreciation you are assuming the perception of your divinity. This allows you to experience the love and beauty that has been here all along, awaiting your vibrational congruence with it.

This is one of the most lucrative 'get rich quick' plans you can endorse for your human journey. Keeping in heart there is nothing more valuable than how you feel, the quickest way to truly feel rich in your life is to acknowledge what you can be grateful for *now* in your life.

The soul purpose of choosing to be grateful is to feel better. The feeling of gratitude and appreciation is activated by looking deliberately for what is working in your life and what you are grateful for.

Is there anything more divinely decadent than to appreciate your life?

Gratitude is a very powerful antidote to depression and is at the core of mental health and emotional wellbeing. It will support a positive attitude and healthy disposition in life and most importantly allow you to be present for the current blessings in your life, which is the *ultimate* gift.

With everything in life being based in energy and vibration, the highest vibration you can offer is that of appreciation, which is also aligned with the energy of pure love. What you focus on expands, which metaphysically implies that what you appreciate, appreciates!

When you choose to be grateful for your life, you step into a cathedral of consciousness and become a conduit to receive cooperative relationships. Well-being will stream into your life in a myriad of ways, courtesy of the Divine Conspiracy collaborating with your free will. The 'Universal Banking System' will pay out massive dividends to you when you choose to be a yay-sayer and play angel's advocate for your life.

Each time you make a conscious choice (yes it is a choice!) to acknowledge what you are grateful for and what is working in your life, you will receive more to be grateful for, courtesy of the neutral omnipotent Law of Response. This natural law assures that there is a gravitational pull to your consciousness and you are attracting based on how you feel.

In material terms, the residual benefit of focusing on what you are grateful for will be *more to be grateful for* and the manifestation of your heart's desires.

The important distinction here is you won't need these things to come into your experience in order to feel good and grateful. You will have already cultivated an inner affluence based on your focus of attention to be on appreciation and what you are grateful for.

You will be liberated from the co-dependency of the external and free from the cultural "If/Then - When/Then" epidemic. This epidemic has had your emotional well being contingent on, and tethered to, something outside of yourself which is at the core of suffering - needing something or someone to change in order to be happy.

Waiting for your life to meet your ego's illusive standards before you are grateful, is an expensive layaway plan for your happiness that will never pay off.

Remembering you are creating from the inside out, as a vibrational being on 'vibrationalmatch.com' you must first create an internal state of well being and fulfillment in order for your external reality to improve and mirror that back to you.

Radical gratitude is the ability to be grateful for things in your life that you may have defined as challenges, circumstances or events that are 'bad' or have gone 'wrong'.

When you become grateful for all of the highs, lows, and in-betweens, you release the anger and resentment due to what you previously perceived as *life happening to you,* and can begin to see the golden thread and silver lining in these experiences.

It is often easier to be grateful for the things that are going 'right' according to your ego's standards, however 'radical gratitude' initiates another level of depth and evolution of consciousness as you are witnessing your trials and tribulations within your Soul's graduate program.

Viewing your challenges through the following inspired interrogations and 'quest- ions', allows you to transmute defiant energies and radically improve how you are feeling.

- How is this experience serving my greater awareness?

- How is this a blessing in disguise guiding me to a life of greater authenticity and purpose?

- How would love and compassion perceive this experience?

- These life affirming quest-ions will initiate miracles and soulutions for you as this intentional inquiry is an essential note in the higher octave of your spiritual perspective in this lifetime. Interpreting your trying experiences as divine catalysts for your empowerment will allow you to step into greater mastery and align with your soul's beneficial intent.

There is no experience in your life that cannot be utilized as a catalyst to open your heart to your own Divinity and elevate your states of consciousness. When you become grateful for everything that is unfolding in your life, even that which you have deemed a 'challenge', you become a sacred alchemist.

Get Rich Quick

Most of us have been exposed to conventional 'get rich quick schemes' which suggest that miracles occur without our vibrational participation.

These illusive schemes perpetuate the costly illusion that our lives will improve through external conditions - when we get " the thing' - "out there". Putting your emotional well being on the 'layaway plan' - paid in full when you are rescued and saved.

A deliberate gratitude practice will allow you to be inner resourced, affording you the opportunity to truly 'get rich quick' emotionally. This is a powerful gesture of self love and your 'ticket' to winning the internal lottery!

Your life will blossom in the most fragrant of ways as you remember the true essence and genesis of being R.I.C.H. - "Realizing I Create Happiness".

As we can see in the spiritual etymology of language - Thank you. Your welcome (your well will come).

Get Rich Quick Practice / Mental Fitness Gym/Spa

"I wish I hadn't done my gratitude practice!" said no one ever! :)

A deliberate gratitude practice is a course requirement to 'earn' your P.H.D. (personal happiness degree) in the graduate program of the Elite University of your life.

This gratitude practice literally saved my life and guided me from being penniless and feeling pointless to feeling positive expectation and hopefulness, ultimately lending itself to my true sense of Self and soul's purpose. This practice became the 'tributary' in the divine flow, now connecting me with you, in service to your journey, of which I am so grateful.

Even amidst the pitch black night of my Soul, I chose to begin to look at all of the things that I DID have in my life and be grateful for them. It was not easy at first to notice what was working in my life, as my primary focus had been on what was lacking. This light felt like a fleeting flicker at first, but was sufficient enough, as light always is.

All it takes is a single gratitude candle to spark and illuminate a path to greater well being and peace. The more I did the practice of gratitude, the easier it became and now I can't imagine my life without an integral basecamp of gratitude. It is the primary reason that I am still upright on the planet and offering these words to you.

Keep in mind and heart, no matter how bad your life may seem, you have the ability to reach for a thought that feels better in any given moment and in doing so, raise your vibration, which will invite opportunities in response to your elevated mood. Feeling better and emotional shifts occur at the speed of thought.

As you shift focus to what feels better, you will immediately begin to feel better. Remembering that in this vibrational magnetic paradise in which you feel, you are attracting based on how you feel. The better you feel, the better your life will get and the better it gets, the better you will feel.

You will be liberated from the dysfunctional notion that you will 'believe it when you see it' and be fortified in the metaphysical reminder that you are seeing based on what you believe. You will 'buy in' to your own state of empowerment and ability to affect positive change in your life.

Your appreciation muscle may have atrophied, however it still exists and is eager to begin its divine reps to strengthen your connection with your true Self.

There are three choices when it comes to your 'Get Rich Quick' gratitude practice. Each choice will be emotionally lucrative for you.

Your practice can consist of-

1. Thinking thoughts of appreciation
2. Speaking appreciation
3. Writing appreciation

When you *think* a thought of gratitude, you are triggering one synapse in your mind, which is equivalent to offering one vibrational request. This is singularly powerful.

When you *speak* appreciation, you are triggering two synapses and offering two requests- which is doubly powerful.

When you *write*, it is triple powerful. Writing down what you are grateful for is the most powerful because you are initiating a 'ceremony'. A ceremony is simply when you unite an intention with an action.

The intention is to be grateful. The action is to write it down. Your invitation is to begin a deliberate *gratitude journal* practice.

For true sustainable shifts to occur you must do the practice the majority of the time, which is at least 4 days a week. This will foster momentum courtesy of physics and the Law of Momentum. The invitation is to write at least 4 days a week, 3 things that you are grateful for. It can be about absolutely anything.

> *You will know you are doing the exercise correctly because it will feel good to do so.*

Ideally you will begin this practice at the beginning of your day because this will set the energetic tone for your day, however trust yourself to find a time that is easiest for you. Consistency pays, and is key to allow the new and improved neural pathways to be forged.

The purpose of this practice is to FEEL appreciation. It takes approximately 17 seconds to activate a new vibration so you will want to linger on each grateful aspect for at least 30 seconds. This will allow the feeling to reverberate and resonate in your being.

The key is to also do your best to not repeat yourself. If you are repeating the same thing over and over, it will start to feel 'generic', so it is important to look for something new. As you go on a deliberate hunt for these refreshing nuances and elements of what you appreciate in your life, you begin to deepen and expand what you are noticing.

As you deepen and expand what you are noticing, the Law of Response will continue to deepen and expand what it brings into your life. What you focus on expands. What you appreciate, appreciates, which will enrich your life more powerfully than ever before.

As you get more practiced, begin to integrate the subjects in your life that you have felt most challenged by. The reason you feel challenged is due to habitually viewing that aspect of your life through the lens of scarcity and what isn't working.

The next time you feel something challenges you at your core, ask how this experience is serving your higher awareness. How might it be catalyzing greater divine attributes of compassion, empathy, forgiveness and love?

When you shift your focus to gratitude you will initiate greater flow and fulfillment in this area of your life. Keep in mind you are not instantly manifesting, and are given a grace period and a buffer. This means in terms of material reflections, it will take approximately 3-4 weeks before new evidence out pictures in your life.

Ultimately you will become so masterful at this that you will realize that there is no such thing as a 'challenge'. Challenges are essentially disguised opportunities to shift from deficit and scarcity mentality into an abundant mindset of gratitude.

Once this practice becomes first nature, everything else will automagically fall into place. As you continue to do this practice consistently, your life will be enriched always and in all ways.

By choosing to see life through the lens of gratitude you bear witness to the beauty that has been here all along, becoming the change you wish to see in the world. As a beacon of gratitude you energetically encourage this inspiration for others. Gratitude is the gift that keeps on giving.

May every day be thanksgiving in the fruitful season of your life. It is incredibly fulfilling to celebrate the gifts in your life, by choosing to see life through the lens of gratitude. When you bear witness to the beauty that has been here all along through this lens, you consummate your devotion to the beauty way, and the gift of your existence.

If there is only one prayer you say each day, may it be "thank you".

CHAPTER SIXTEEN

THE POWER OF YOUR PERCEPTION

*M*any have lived at the whim of external forces, living a life of reaction due to feeling powerless to the circumstances of their life.

It is vital to recognize that there are nearly 8 billion personal realities happening simultaneously. Your perception and beliefs are not responsible for your neighbors reality, no more than your neighbor are responsible for your personal reality.

Your real-eyes-ation of the influence of your perceptions INforming your personal reality is the basis for your sovereignty and for the beneficial motto of humanity - 'live and let live'.

> *When you remember that your perceptions and beliefs inform your emotions/vibrations and you are attracting based on how you feel, this allows the liberating acknowledgement of the importance of minding your own joyful business and tending to the fertile garden of your own mind. The grass is always greener where you water it.*

Loving reminder that your greatest commodity is your attention and what you focus on is expanding (courtesy of the Law of Response). You can now directly relate this understanding to the primary influence of your perception in creating your personal reality.

Essentially everything (literally) that is evidenced in your life now, has shown up as a reflection of the predominant perceptions you have held up until approximately 30 days ago. (Remember things are not instantly manifesting. There is an approximate 30-day grace period between your primary beliefs/thoughts and when they out-picture in your experience).

Arriving at the vital understanding that your perception is the source of how your personal reality is being created, allows you to acknowledge that the origin of "Have vs. Have Not" resides merely in your perception.

This understanding becomes the source of your liberation, security and fulfillment, for you will no longer be a victim to circumstance, or that life is happening to you, but instead, can become the conscious creator of your reality through how you choose to perceive.

You will also be liberated from the dysfunctional notion that you will 'believe it when you see it' and be fortified in the metaphysical reminder that you are *seeing based on what you believe.*

Simply stated, *Your Perception Creates Your Reality.* Your perception shows up in 4 distinct categories – Your *Relationships, Health, Career and Money.* You essentially have two choices regarding how you choose to perceive your life in each of these 4 categories.

You can choose to perceive your life through the lens of lack, scarcity and what isn't working ("Deficit Mentality"), in which case you will create pain, drama and challenges.

This is how powerful you are, courtesy of the Law of Response, neutrally delivering to you more of what you are focused upon.

Your second choice is to perceive your life through the lens of possibility, appreciation and what is working ("Abundant Mentality"), in which case you will create infinite possibilities and more to appreciate. This is how powerful you are, courtesy of the Law of Response neutrally delivering to you more of what you are focused upon.

As you acknowledge that your perception is responsible for your reality, and your reality consists of your relationships, health, money and career, you are able to liberate yourself from the misunderstanding that anything external will provide you with fulfillment, security, freedom and peace, because your reality is an extension of your perception.

This also frees you from the *"If Then/When Then"* epidemic. *If* I make a certain amount of money, then I will be secure. *When I* meet a partner, *then* I will feel love. *When I* get a raise, *then I* will feel valuable. *If I* lose 10 pounds, *then* I will be happy.

Remembering there is a gravitational pull to your consciousness that is validating your inner dialogue with people, circumstances and situations, your experiences are merely reflections of your previous predominant perceptions, out-picturing and evidencing themselves in your current reality.

> *Knowing that you are attracting based on how you feel in this magnetic paradise in which you live, you can then real-eyes that the very seeking of something outside of yourself for an experience of fulfillment and peace, is inherently flawed.*

The very seeking implies your current state of lack and dismisses the metaphysical truth that you are always on vibrationalmatch.com. *You are creating from the inside out, therefore freedom, security, fulfillment and peace is all an inside job.*

The most prominent representation of this hallucination in our culture today resides in the pursuit of "Financial Freedom". As you integrate this reminder into the subject of money, you can apply the same foundational understanding that your perception is informing your reality, and in this specific case your reality of money, as well as your experience of freedom.

Money itself is innocent. Most people view money as if it is it's own entity, running around with arms and legs, having power over people's lives and informing their experience, of which they have little to no influence.

If you choose to perceive that money is the source of your freedom, you will live your life in accordance with that belief, in constant pursuit of this and never realizing it. It is only from a place of recognizing and therefore experiencing freedom in your current life-exactly how it is-that you are able to activate that feeling of freedom.

Being in pursuit of freedom on an external level, merely feeds the illusion of financial freedom, once again, recognizing that you are attracting based on how you feel. Money cannot buy you happiness, but you can buy money through the currency of your own joy and wellbeing. As you continue the lucrative awareness of the power of your perception, you will begin to wonder why you ever limited your state of abundance by focusing on your bank account.

When you assume the feeling of freedom in your current life exactly how it is, by deliberately placing your attention on the subjects that feel good now, you will activate that vibration of freedom. The energetic result of that in the form of manifestation, will be money, however it is not responsible for your freedom, but rather an energetic byproduct and extension of your already existing experience of freedom.

Coming back to the foundational understanding of the influence of your perception in creating your reality, a perception that is based in scarcity and lack, will have you constantly in pursuit of something to fill that. It's impossible to be fulfilled in that state, because your reality can only shift when you shift your perception.

This lends itself to Einstein's quote – "Insanity is doing the same thing and expecting a different result." The true insanity is thinking your results and your reality will change from action alone. The only way to change your reality is by shifting your perception.

It is an integral piece and a game changer to discover that the true origin of any degree of scarcity, pain and drama in your life, originates from misaligned thinking and from a misaligned perception, and focusing your greatest commodity – your attention, on lack and what isn't working.

> *You should feel an incredible amount of relief in simply knowing that in order to improve your life, all that is required is for you to shift your perception to what is working and what you appreciate regarding the subjects where you are currently experiencing pain, drama and challenges.*

As you shift your inner ratio of attention from 49 to 51% from the perception of challenge to a perception of possibility regarding those subjects, the Law of Momentum will handle the rest. In a short amount of time (approximately 30 days), your outer world will become a reflection of that internal shift. Evidence will show up in the form of solutions, possibilities and more to appreciate. This is once again all courtesy of the neutral omnipotent Law of Response, which is delivering to you more of what you are focused on. It is important to acknowledge and affirm this manifestation as it arises in your life, as your mind loves to see the evidence of its effect in your reality.

In addition to what is showing up in your experience, let's also return to the most vital aspect of your life, which is how you feel. When you choose to place your attention on what is working in your life and reach for appreciation regarding the areas where you are experiencing pain and drama, you immediately feel better, and are therefore already a winner.

You now have the opportunity to bring in a new definition for the word "challenges". As you realize the true source of your power and reclaim it by noticing and acknowledging that your perception is creating your reality, there inherently is never really a true challenge in your life.

> *Challenges are really just disguised opportunities for you to shift your perception regarding the subject that you are currently experiencing pain and drama.*

Every challenge in your life then becomes an incredible opportunity to shift the inner ratio of your attention from one of lack, scarcity and not-enough-ness, to a focus on what IS working, possibilities and appreciation (which is the highest vibration you can offer).

As you real-eyes that any experience of pain and drama is merely a result of misaligned thinking, you will no longer be a victim and at the whim of life, but rather, you will live in a world of true accountability and true responsibility as a deliberate and magnificent creator.

Your experience then becomes an opportunity, born from compassionate awareness, for you to clean up your perception and to visit those subjects that you subscribed to the illusion of lack and scarcity, and return to greater love and appreciation for what is.

Your thoughts give rise to your feelings, which inform your actions, which produce your results. The genesis and origin of your results resides in your predominant thoughts and perceptions.

This is one of the fundamental elements in claiming your power in all aspects of your life and shifting your reality. Regardless of what you are currently experiencing, you can rest assured it will positively shift and improve as your perception elevates.

CHAPTER SEVENTEEN

THE POWER OF YOUR IMAGINATION

*Y*our past only defines you if you keep talking about it and focusing on it. One of the greatest resources you have been gifted is your imagination, which is the birth place of your soon to be reality. Your future experience is INformed by the stories that you tell yourself today.

The Universe is responding to your vibration which is activated by what you are focusing on now, and now and now. There is no distinction between your past and the future.

Many people retell old stories that do not feel good and use the powerful commodity of their internal storyboard to imagine all of the things that could go wrong. This is a costly tarmac to launch your future from, because the foundation of this planet is a vibrational one.

Telling the same stories that do not feel good to you, will assure the same results, as your thoughts and consciousness are the genesis of your personal reality. History and herstory repeats itself when we regurgitate the same stories over and over, which is why things do not fundamentally change. The energetics stay the same, but are presented in different packages of characters and circumstances.

> *Be mindful to not get caught up in focusing on what 'is' and what is evidenced in your current reality and circumstances. Today's manifestation is yesterday's vibration. To create a new reality for yourself, you must spend more time imagining and less time reacting.*

If you do decide to go down memory lane, do so with an honoring inquiry, appreciating all that has come to pass, in favor of your evolution and your journey home to Self.

To birth a new reality - you must predominantly hold the desired vision for what you are wanting, and begin to focus your attention there and to begin to tell a better feeling story - beginning with yourSelf. This will In-form a new paradigm and new reality that is beneficial.

Wishful thinking is very resourceful as it is grounded in a state of hopefulness and appreciation and you are attracting based on how you feel. Never believe a prediction from your mind that doesn't empower you.

Are you imagining what can go right? Or what will go wrong? Is Murphy's Law in effect: 'anything that can go wrong, will go wrong'. Or is Your law in effect - "Anything that can go right, can and does!"

The future belongs to those that believe in the beauty of their dreams. Your belief in your dreams is a necessary energetic component to foster the vibration that will allow all cooperative components to assist in the realization of our New Earth.

Stay focused on the essence of what you are wanting to feel. You can begin with the 'wouldn't it be nice if.....' game. This is a powerful energetic bridge to walk upon as you begin to entertain the notion of something new and delightful to come into your experience.

Relinquish the 'who, how, when and where', and allow those details to be summoned by your team of allies, and the orchestration of Infinite Intelligence. Remember Spirit can dream a dream far more fulfilling for you than you can imagine for yourself.

Stay open to how the magic will unfold for you as you INjoy the creative journey of fulfillment in collaboration with the energy that breathes you and creates worlds.

CHAPTER EIGHTEEN

THE CONVENIENT TRUTH

One of the major causes of dis-ease and despair is a sense of worry and powerlessness regarding the health of our beloved planet and the injustices in the world.

During this time of Great Decision it is essential to remember that our ENvironment is an outpicturing of our INvironment. Everything is a reflection. The personal *is* reflected in the planetary.

> *The experience of pain, drama and dis-ease on our planet has been a by-product of the majority of the planet being asleep to their essential power and being governed predominantly by fear - up until now.*

In considering whether you are part of the soulution or part of the pollution, it is important to remember the essence of "be the change you wish to see in the world", which is in-formed by your state of *being* and vibration. Your contribution to our planetary wellness is derived from your state of consciousness, which is governed by where you are placing your attention and your inner dialogue.

Even with the best intentions, many people (including environmentalists and activists) are 'doing the change' at their own expense - feeling depleted and overwhelmed, with their actions carrying the energetic signature of fear and scarcity with an emphasis on what isn't working.

> *Everything we do will bear the mark of the consciousness in which we do it. To incite true change and soulutions, we must recall that everything*

is an outpicturing of the relationship we have with ourselves and our core beliefs.

When we choose to shift our limiting beliefs from fear, lack and scarcity into one of trust and love, and focus primarily on what *is* working, our planet and our world will reflect this back to us.

When we are coming from the base camp of joy, trust, hopefulness and inspiration,we are genuinely in service to sustainable beneficial shifts for the planet and all of Her inhabitants.

Our actions become reactions when derived from fear, despair and frustration. From this place nothing fundamentally shifts, as is evidenced in our results up until now. This energy will perpetuate more pain and more drama. Desperate times don't call for desperate measures, they call for inspired measures.

It is vital to recall that problems can not be solved by the same consciousness in which they were created, and insanity is doing the same thing over and over and expecting different results. True insanity is thinking our results will change from action alone. No amount of action can compensate for fear based thinking.

Today's results and what is evidenced in our world, reflects our previous focus. What we are experiencing now personally and collectively is dictated by our predominant beliefs up until approximately 3-4 weeks ago.

Manifestation is thankfully not instantly occurring. Imagine how chaotic our lives would be if our thoughts instantly manifested? We are given a grace period and a buffer which allows us the opportunity to curate our beliefs, and shift the focus of our attention on best case scenarios and play angels advocate for ourselves, each other and for our planet.

There is a sequence of manifestation which governs the migratory pattern of beliefs and focus into evidence. This migratory timeline is approximately 3-4 weeks. Our thoughts give rise to our feelings which inform our actions which produce our results.

When we connect these energetic dots, we can real-eyes that the greatest environmental act begins with our awareness of where we are putting our attention and what we are focusing on. The greatest revolution is always catalyzed from within.

Awareness of any issues or challenges is important *to a degree* and is the greatest facilitator for change, however we must remember that what we focus on expands. We must be vigilant and aware of our inner ratio of attention and to not have the majority of our focus going towards the issue or challenge. This will promote a daunting, defeating and overwhelming feeling which will disrupt our alignment to the solutions, as we are attracting based on how we feel.

Not feeling good is our INdicator that we are in opposition to beneficial outcomes. All soulutions reside downstream in the inherent current of well-being which is governed by the Ultimate orchestrator of life itself.

It is vital to have the majority of our focus on what is working, the essence of what we are wanting for our results and towards possibilities. This will INsure a feeling of inspiration, which will instigate solutions to include all of the cooperative relationships to create a beneficial outcome for all beings. This is the energetic template for true sustainable shifts, and to resolve the current challenges that we face.

INjustices occur when we lose sight of our true nature and our interconnection with all beings and with all life. When we remember that our personal lives are informed by our beliefs and vibration and not from the external world, we are able to liberate ourselves from victim consciousness and the 'blame game'. When we buy into the notion of lack and scarcity, we begin to fight for our 'share' and begin to feel powerless as we mind the business of others.

If we subscribe to the notion that other people influence our reality and our well being, we succumb to victim consciousness and activate a feeling of powerlessness. What we believe becomes so, so if we do believe we are influenced by another, so shall it be.

At the core of the dis-ease on our planet is the notion of lack and scarcity, however when we remember the Universal ploy of well being and the divine currency, we will receive abundant payouts based on our "free will" involvement of an aligned vibration.

Bringing awareness to these issues through literal marching and campaigning can be somewhat effective, however, because what we focus on expands, if we continue to focus on what is 'wrong', what is lacking and what isn't working, we will perpetuate more of the same in the world of results.

> We must march to the front lines of our consciousness and go within and have an honest look at the ultimate perpetrator, which is our own fears and scarcity mentality. We must attend to our mental hygiene as much as our dental hygiene in order to clean up the pollutants 'out there'. Remembering we are creating from within and from our own vibrations, this allows us to relinquish vestibules of codependency, and stand in our sovereignty.

Sovereignty is standing resilient within our own being, not buying into the illusion that our security, happiness and fulfillment is governed by or resides in an outside agency. Those that are sovereign recognize that this state of core alignment with our true identity reigns supreme, in our ability to operate not from a place of co-dependency but radiantly in our interdependence with all of life.

When we choose to have deep reverence for our essential Self and connect with our true identity of love and light, we are able to foster compassion and understanding of our soul's journey. This affords us compassion and graces us with the ability to foster empathy and compassion for the other fellow travelers that cross our path.

When we are triggered or feel judgement, we can acknowledge that each person becomes a reflection, mirroring for us where we can return to greater love and compassion within ourselves. This Higher Self- fullness choice will continue to promote a massive R.O.I. - ripple of impact in our lives and is the Ultimate form of caretaking our planet.

Certain African traditions believed that a song would summon the soul to arrive before birth. This individual's soul song was sung only on two other occasions -at the time of death to assist their transition into the next chapter of existence, and if the person 'forgot themSelves' and committed a crime or did harm to another.

Instead of punishing, shaming and extricating the individual, they were brought into the center of the circle of their community and the village would sing their soul song to them. This would activate a remembrance of the truth of who they are and the knowing that as we do unto others we do unto ourselves.

> Goodwill can fully arise as we begin to fully own the privilege of who we innately are on a soulular level, unified through loving intent, each with a signature skin suit by the epic designer of Source and God.

Everything is a mirror. Look at your own life which is a microcosm of the macrocosm. Has anything beneficial come from fear? All good things evolve from love.

When we choose to love ourselves first and our neighbors second, we cultivate a state of well being that will catalyze inspiration. These inspirational shifts will automagically unfold in a world of soulution, collaboration and a vibrant planet that honors all manifestations of the ever present source of love.

For those that are on a mission in service to others and are feeling overwhelmed in your endeavors, it is vital to remember that Lighthouses do not go looking for boats that are lost at sea. They stand in their resilience serving as a beacon to illuminate the way to safety. So glow on luminous being, minding your own joyful business as a vibrational beacon inspiring others to honor and amplify their own wattage.

True service generates from being attentive to our vibrational offering and emotional signature within our mission. Assure that you are representing the true template of this existence which begins with Self care and Self love. Past martyrdom and self sabotage serves as a powerful contrast to acknowledge what hasn't fundamentally worked.

As vibrational beings that attract based on how we feel, when we choose to focus on gratitude and what is working we shift 'doom and gloom' into the 'gratitude and bloom' movement.

From a state of deliberate gratitude, focusing on what is working, and operating from trust, we will then realize and create many tangible solutions that will resolve any dis-ease that is happening on our planet.

Yesterday I was clever and wanted to change the world, today I am wise and am choosing to love myself fully and focus on what is working in my life and in the world.

CHAPTER NINETEEN

COPING WITH THE 'LOSS' OF A LOVED ONE

*M*any beings leave the stage of their life in a manner that may leave you with a cry of agony in your heart as the fragile thread of your faith is dealt with so violently.

Is anyone strong enough to stay conscious through an experience such as this? Probably very few.

And even they would only have a whisper of equanimity and peace amidst their rage, grief, horror and desolation.

I can not lessen your pain with any words, nor should I. For your pain is their legacy to you. Not that they would inflict such pain by choice, but there it is, and it must burn it's purifying way to completion.

For something in you dies when you bear the unbearable, and it is only in that dark night of your soul that you are prepared to see as the Divine sees, and to love as Source does.

Let your grief find expression. No false strength. Meet it with grace and acceptance.

Now is the time to sit quietly and speak to your loved one and thank them for being with you during the time that you shared.

Encourage them to go on with their service and work, knowing that you will grow in compassion and wisdom from this experience.

Know that you will commune and meet with them again and again, and recognize the many ways in which you have known each other.

And when you meet you will know, in a flash, what now is not given to you to know - why this had to be the way it was.

Your rational mind will never understand what has happened, but your heart –when you keep it open— will find its own intuitive way.

Now your loved one's soul is free, and the love that you have shared is invulnerable to the winds of changing time and space, and the illusion of separation.

May your union with Spirit and the essence of all that is hold you, and provide a healing salve for your heart.

Surrender into the arms of the Divine Mother, knowing that she is nestled within your darkest moments —anointing and gracing your heart with an infinite knowing of the eternal union you share with your loved ones, always and in all ways.

Let go of any judgement you have towards yourself or them, for this will allow the deepest irrevocable connection of love to permeate your existence forever more.

Bless yourself and your loved ones by letting go of guilt and shame.

Their presence will be known and felt by you through the vessel of your open heart.

They will exist everywhere where joy and love reside.

Adaptation of Ram Dass by Laura Fredrickson

https://www.ramdass.org/

CHAPTER TWENTY

A PRAYER FOR THOSE THAT WALK THE EARTH

A prayer for all of us who walk the Earth.

May I be humble
may I be innocent
may I be wise.

May I know the deep calm of the earth
that glows in the eye of the fox
and that sings with the water bird
rising to beat jewels of light from her wings.

May I be still enough for natural dignity to arise within me
guiding my hand in action and my voice in speech.

May I carry my ancient heart lightly and with real sincerity
knowing that the life that beats within
is as old as forever,
honoured and perfectly wedded
to the ever-arising source of existence.

As I remember my heart
may I see that source within all things
in the eyes of my sacred enemy, my friends and my family,
in green feathers, in white bone and in twisted branches.

Give me the courage to stand as if I am witness to all creation
and to know that all creation is looking back at me,
from stone and child and salt sea-shell spiral.

Grant me the presence to carry my heartbreak well,
and that the pain gives me tenderness and wisdom
so that I may love more deeply
and dance more freely,
walking lightly across the plains and mountains and cities
of this great garden earth.

May my eyes be lifted to the light and
my animal feet strong and bright,
pacing in the freedom of my birth-right
and the effortless nobility of true belonging.

As I walk, may I remember the eyes of old men dying and women
birthing,
the trust of children sleeping and the endless faith of flowers.

Show me how to make every strange feeling and breakdown
a ragged sail to carry my wretched, foundering ship further across the
great ocean
towards the safe harbour of the one love.

May I tread the landscapes of grief with an open chest
drawing meaning from tears and resilience from sadness.

May I recognise mercy
and bow down at the merciless altar
where everything is asked for
and everything is surrendered.

Give me miracles in the ordinary
and humility in the miraculous.

Let the fire at the centre of myself
that burns bright as essence
warm me in the night
and may I never fear its heat
but rather draw close
so that what is not mine burns away like dry grass
revealing new growth green shoots and swelling buds
perpetually opening into the light of now.

May I know how to lie down with myself
and unfold intimacy, my cheek resting on my own perfect silence.

May I remember the plains of darkness between the stars
and the great tapestry of time
through which I dream and which dreams through me.

Grant that I be quiet enough to be able to hear the flowers opening
And wild enough to fly with dragonflies in the textured sunlight.

May I cease to seek for perfection
And recognise the love that is inherent in this simple life,
moving in smiling gratitude
for everything that is given.

For everything truly is given,
breath to breath
heartbeat to heartbeat
life to death.

Unveil the moment and the love that was never hidden
giving love, living love
gentle, strong and brave,
open, alive and just as fully human as this soul can be.

May good seeds sprout as I pass
to sow the life of the future
that will nourish my children
with a rich harvest.

May forests of love grow from doubt
and hate blossom into faith and flowers.

May dignity arise like the sun on a new day
turning the autumn dew to green, red and blue light diamonds,
simple beauty that gives everything
and asks for nothing in return,
for nothing is more precious than gold,
and the empty chest that is full of wonder.

May all beings be at peace.
May you be whole.

In all possible ways
may you be whole.

Ben Bushill

https://www.benbushill.com/

SECTION TWO

WINGING IT INNERVIEWS

WINGING IT PREFACE

*T*he following InnerViews were conducted without premeditation or prior preparation, and were carried on the wings of the divine.

Some of the InnerViews were done with people who work directly with spirit councils and guides.

Jill Jackson & Solomun

Lorcan O'Toole

Yasmeen Clark & Raman Pascha

Some may refer to themselves as "mediums" , which are intuitives that have the ability to communicate and receive messages from the spirit realm.

They serve as a bridge to translate 5D messages into our 3D material plane for the purpose of greater connection, understanding and support from these invisible benevolent beings.

These individuals are able to receive messages through varying senses from a multidimensional storage unit of wisdom.

Consider a channel to be a conduit to receive. One of the important distinctions when thinking of 'channels' is that we are ALL channels.

We all have access to guides and benevolent spirits, however in order to receive a clear signal and pure message it is vital to not have "static" on the line.

This clarity of wisdom and support from the Spirit realm is graced to all that set forth an agreement field with their guides, are able to raise their vibration to be congruent with the Spirit realm, and have purity of intent.

One of the first mental prisons we enter into in our life is our fear of death. This is one of the most misunderstood and misrepresented experiences causing a lot of torment for humans during their journey, and heartache regarding the perceived 'loss' of loved ones that have crossed over and transitioned.

My intention for the InnerViews that involve the mediums, is to offer a deeper understanding of what *really* occurs when we cross over. May this offer you solace as you remember the many dimensions of love and the ultimate recycling program of energy.

The chapters -'Annie' and 'Catherine' are beautiful examples of how your loved ones will continue to connect with you in unexpected ways, to remind you that you are always held and supported during your journey.

The "Divine Assignment" chapter will support you to open your channel to stay connected to your loved ones if you so choose, and to be receptive to the myriad of ways they will continue to bless you with their presence and love.

WINGING IT WITH BENJAMIN

Laura:

What would you say to someone who is struggling and considering ending their life?

Benjamin:

This is a unique opportunity to be present in human form. Whatever its circumstances —a life of ease or challenges, a life of privilege or poverty— how precious is this experience to simply be present here in form, to be in the body, in the heart and with the love we bear for the people in our lives.

As it is understood to be in many traditions, to share love with the people in your life is oh so precious — the Buddha said it was just one in millions and millions of degrees of possibility and probability to be in a human form, so this is a deep ancient teaching.

There is also an opportunity each morning to reinvent oneself and one's relationship with life, and not be caught up in old frameworks or patterns or conditioned ideas. The opportunity is there to be fresh in the moment, to reconsider and reinvent, and to do so with a profound gift of love with oneself and others.

This core love can be the seed that plants the possibilities of a new vision. It becomes the nourishing source that can feed into a new opening and some new direction, that core of love.

One of the interesting things about life is that we identify so heavily with a role, we identify so heavily with a storyline or narrative, and when that narrative for some reason turns down, we identify continually with it and feel somehow a sense of defeat, or a sense of despair — when really it's just the narrative turning down.

If we are willing to note that we are ultimately the author of that narrative, that we are really the ones holding that pen, then we don't have to remain contained in an old narrative, in an old set of ideas or an old set of measures and ideals about our worth. That affords us a new page that each day brings.

Laura:

Have you ever considered ending your life?

Benjamin:

I had one experience of being in my body that was intolerable, like a fragment or thorn in my side, when I felt 'at risk' for this outcome. Since then I have thought about suicide and have related to others through the lens of the feeling of being unable to remain in the body.

At the precipice, this pushes into the experience of running out of space to exist in, feeling so pushed out of arriving in your body. It can be like carrying out a metaphor - the psychic experience of not being able to take up space and time in this life. It was during a nihilistic period in my teens, before I had seen into a deeper reality. A dark period.

Years after that I had the numinous experience of seeing the deeper truth and a sacred experience of reality. The core of my suffering during that time of darkness was centered around the meaning — is life purposeful on the whole? Struggling to find the larger sense of purposefulness of being here, in the larger context does all of it have a purpose and a meaning? Ultimately this existential crisis was resolved by seeing into the numinous, sacred dimension of life —beyond the material-- where patterns of meaning and purpose infuse what we see playing out in front of our eyes.

Once the glimpse occurred it resolved many things. Having just one experience of seeing the deep pattern of purposefulness, it was enough —even if I hadn't had it for a long time following— it was enough for me to set my view of it straight. I could feel that it was the deeper sense of the world. I was with a Sufi teacher, reading a dream he had to a circle of friends. I had a direct experience of the dream while reading it — I was 'him' having his dream. It allowed me to see what was being described very vividly — more real than waking life. In the dream he was given a tour of the nature of reality and I got to ride on the coat-tails of his experience, which in turn became my experience.

The soul places many experiences in our path —some beautiful, some painful or difficult— intended to serve or summon our learning and growing. Looking at our lives, we can see the pattern these things placed in our way to prod us towards self understanding. As I look at my own soul's intention for my life, I can see it is pushing me to release the play of the world completely enough to experience my own true nature — to let go of roles and conditioning and attachments to know what is real.

- Benjamin

WINGING IT WITH
JILL JACKSON & SOLOMUN

Laura:

What would you share with someone who is considering ending their life?

Jill:

We as guides honour and value each soul's free will option for each incarnation.

We would encourage each individual's soul to seek every avenue possible as there are so many, both in this realm and the other realms, ready and open to embrace the challenges sometimes brought upon by these very dense dimensions.

We would also encourage each lovely being that is struggling that they remember that they do have their own special guides and spirit team that they can communicate with at will, at any time to assist them with these challenges.

We would also ask them to remember that any challenges they are experiencing in each incarnation, their soul not only agreed to these experiences but actually welcomed them prior to incarnating.

Sometimes once we are in the physical body, the density of this vibration and the challenges seem to be overwhelming in a way that is different from the higher dimensions when we are looking at our life plan and our soul contracts.

We lovingly understand this. Each soul who may be experiencing challenges can certainly communicate with their spirit team and their guides and ask for these challenges to be mitigated, to transmute them in a way that can be better handled in this incarnation.

We also love and honour each soul's freewill who may choose to leave prior to the ending of their soul contract; however we must lovingly remind each one of you that it is the soul's expression to evolve, not only in each lifetime but life between life and in the other realms.

It is the soul's evolution to continue to expand and through each of life's challenges comes expansion. We would ask each one of you to remember the beauty because sometimes it is darkest right before the dawn. If we can assist each one of you through these challenges to expand your awareness and to be able to walk with you through these challenges this is mutually beneficial for everyone involved during not only this lifetime, but past lifetimes and future lifetimes as well.

Laura:

For someone who has never had connection with their guides or asked for help in the unseen realm in this way, what is something that they can do to connect and begin to feel supported in this way?

Jill:

We would first invite each one of you to look at any substances being ingested in the physical body because what we have witnessed is there are certain pharmaceuticals and certain medications that are changing the rewiring of the human brain and many times this is contributing to a feeling of chaos, and a feeling of not being able to handle the challenges that are presented from the current lifetime.

We would invite each person to first view that scenario because so many times we are witnessing that those who have chosen to end this physical lifetime that they are in, many, many times it is because of an outside substance such as a pharmaceutical that is not agreeing with the vibration of the soul which is housed in the human body. We would ask the individual person to look at that first and consult with a natural physician - a naturopath.

We are recommending this because there are high vibrating individuals who have chosen to represent the medical field through natural medicine who will be able to work with many of you to help in these situations If this is not the scenario and the individuals are not ingesting a foreign substance, a drug, a pharmaceutical into their physical body and yet they are still feeling like they are not able to handle certain challenges we invite you to pray and to meditate because even though it may feel like you are alone, you are never alone.

Each one of you incarnates with a spirit guide that walks with you and with you at all times. Lovely ones, you are never alone, ever. We are here and we are hearing you. We really invite you to connect and to pray and to meditate and to reach out for help because there is always help. There is always help. We hope that this answers this specific question.

Laura:

Yes. Would the spirit team agree that every disease is a form of suicide?

Jill:

This is a complicated and deep question. What we have witnessed is there are many manifestations of physical disease in the human body. Many of the aspects of these diseases come in from the mental realm however not all of the diseases are coming in from the mental realm, some of the diseases are actually coming in from toxins being created by humans not appreciating Mother Earth and some individuals their physical bodies are affected more than others from outside toxins. It is a very complex and complicated matter to explain in a way that can be understood in the third dimensional vibration.

Laura:

Is there a predetermined death date of this earth journey? We have a birth date, and we have a death date and you had shared earlier that if in our free will we decide to end that earlier that had me wonder if there is a predetermined death date according to the soul's agenda?

Jill:

Again, each individual soul has a separate contract but for the majority of the souls incarnating at this time what we have seen is most souls chose three alternative death dates. This is why we invite certain mediums and psychics maybe not to discuss certain death dates because there are multiple death dates and each individual soul with their free will has these various dates in place.

Yes, there is one final death date that the soul agreed upon. At many times there are near death experiences that come about even on the first or the second death date. While the personality and the ego of the person inhabiting the body, the soul inhabiting the body may not have recollections. Some of you will have recollection of corresponding with your spirit team during these near-death experiences.

It is discussed in a very telepathic manner whether that soul has accomplished what they came here to do. Many times the spirit team will urge that individual to maybe not choose that death date and survive, so to speak in your language, this near-death experience to be able to go back and accomplish more in that physical incarnation. For the majority of souls what we can say is that most chose three.

Laura:

What is the soul's purpose for this earth walk? What is the soul's intention for this journey?

Jill:

Evolution and expansion of the soul. As souls we all crave expansion and evolution. That is what is happening right now in your dimension and there are some souls who chose to incarnate at this time to not only bring in an increased vibration for them individually but also to assist in the mass vibrational accession for Mother Earth.

At the essence, what the soul craves is expansion and being able to grow and evolve to a higher vibrational frequency. Many of the Galactic's that some of you may have been communicating with or listened to through channelling are also vibrating at different frequencies as well. This is a very complex and complicated matter but for the individual soul the craving is evolving and ascending to the higher frequencies.

Laura:

When someone takes their own life what happens behind the veil?

Jill:

This is very individualist as well. What we have witnessed is from the guides standpoint and the loved ones embracing the soul that has chosen to transition prior to one of their soul contract death dates, is the best way that we can put it in your language, there is nothing but love and comfort.

However, we can also explain that what we are witnessing from the individual souls who have made this free will decision, the majority of them feel a sense of sadness and despair because in the moments of making this decision they are immediately in the higher frequencies and are in that moment able to look at their life review and their soul contract that they had agreed on a soul level with their team to accomplish.

Many of them have a period of mourning in this vibration. It's the same in our realm. We are here to assist them through this process. They go through the healing chamber as every soul does once they make their physical transition to the other realms.

There is no difference whether the transition occurs through what you know to be as suicide or what you know to be as physical decline through an illness, where the physical body is shutting down in these ways.

The process is the same through the healing chambers. What we have witnessed is again many souls do go through a period of their own mourning, but it is certainly not anything like what others are saying or preaching in that they all go to what you would call hell. There are only the other worlds and other vibrations and so it is a period of healing and assisting these individuals with the free will choices that they have made.

Laura:

When someone crosses over is it correct to say that there is an element of the personality that sustains in the spirit world?

Jill:

Yes, our dear ones, absolutely. The many facets of the personality are embedded in the DNA. This is why each person may bring forth memories from past lives that are embedded into the frequency of the DNA. So, yes, there are aspects of the personality that do reside with the soul that are there embodied in the field so to speak.

Again our time is much different than your linear time, but in your linear time and the way that you can understand there is a period of the personality of the soul remaining and going through a process of understanding through the soul's process.

This is why mediums will be able to describe the personality of the individual during not only their last lifetime but also past lifetimes as well. This aspect of the personality remains in a stronger way, so to speak directly after their transition.

Laura:

What is the connection between the healing chamber and that resolution, let's say of the personality and the next reincarnation is that intimately connected?

Jill:

It's beautifully woven and intimately connected to, absolutely, our dear ones. As you have counsellors and coaches and psychics and shamans and mediums and channels. We in the other realms have also teams of assistance in these areas. Each soul has a community of team members who assist them.

In a way that we can explain where those of you reading this will be able to understand and those of you listening will be able to understand. It's sort of like going to a counsellor in your realm where we lovingly meet with individual souls and assist them and help them grow.

Again, our dear ones this is free will. A soul has the free will choice not to take advantage so to speak of the opportunities of evolving the soul in the other realms as well. For the majority of souls what we have witnessed is they welcome this beautiful opportunity to continue their evolution of their soul's expansion while in the other realms, waiting and meeting and communicating with their team to make the decision of when and where to reincarnate, what planet, what star system, all of these things.

If it is your earthly planet, what country, what area? There are so many opportunities and so many different things that we as guides help each soul with as long as with their own freewill choice, they ask us for that help. After the healing chamber we meet with each individual soul and we counsel them. it's all telepathic, it's all by energy and vibration but we help them look at their life review.

We help them look at decisions that were made, possibly parts of their soul contract that may not have been completed in this incarnation. These are the types of things that through our meetings, and our healings and our connections we help them choose future incarnations.

Laura:

If someone doesn't fulfil their souls' purpose and exits earlier than their soul contract, is that carried forward in the next incarnation for them to get it then?

Jill:

Again this is a freewill choice but what we have witnessed is the majority of souls crave this evolution. Yes, the majority of souls will choose to continue with the same lessons and growth opportunities that they may have not accomplished in this incarnation, and so they will choose to continue with the same soul growth opportunities in the next incarnation.

Laura:

For someone who is experiencing the loss of a loved one to suicide and is feeliny guilt, shame, devastation and feeling responsible, wondering if they could have done something more, is there anything you would like to share with them? Is there anything you would like to share with those beings?

Jill:

We would invite each person to remain in the vibration of love, and we would remind each one of you that the vibration of guilt does not exist in the higher realms. The vibration of guilt and even sadness and regret are lower frequency vibrations that you have chosen to incarnate in this third dimension at this time experience.

However, in the higher dimensions we do not experience the same type of vibrations. We understand and vibrate with the frequency of love. We remind each one of you as long as you can stay in the vibration of love, this is what your soul is craving in this incarnation. Because when we stay in the frequency of love this is a higher vibration where you can more easily connect with each one of your spirit guides and your angels and your loved ones.

For those of you who have lost loved ones please know they are not lost, this is a human term. Those who have chosen to end their lives earlier than their soul contracts, we invite you not to feel guilt because each soul makes their own freewill choices at each given second and each given moment, of each given time, of each lifetime. There are so many lifetimes.

Please know that your loved ones are not judged. They are not judged in any way. They are supported and they are loved. They are offered healing and loving support with the choices that they have made. We lovingly ask each one of you not to hold onto any guilt because what we have witnessed is your loved ones will go through their own period of feeling certain human emotions right after their transition, because it is so close to the third dimensional frequency that they have maintained parts of the human personality.

However, we work with them to help them transmute any lower vibrational frequencies that are connected to the DNA and part of the soul's signature in a way that we can explain this in terms that we hope you will be able to understand.

Laura:

For the loved ones that are still on earth, is there acceptance of their loved one's choice intimately woven into the healing process?

Jill:

Absolutely because we are all connected. This is another message that we are imploring so many of you to help the masses and help each person understand that yes there is an individual soul however each and every one of you is connected to each and every one of us.

We are elated that your scientists through quantum physics have been able to prove this in a way that many of you who have more of the analytic minds so to speak can understand this scientific exploration. We are elated that this came about but we are each and every one of us are connected, and you, our loved ones, our connected to your loved ones in the other realms.

When you can offer up a higher vibration of forgiveness when you can offer up a higher vibration of understanding and of love then that assists your loved one with their own souls' evolution while also creating an infinite way of raising your own frequency and your own vibration for this life time that you are still experiencing while you are growing and evolving as an individual soul.

So, can you see how infinity is so beautifully interwoven and interconnected and we are so elated that you are asking this question because it is so important for each person that is still in the physical realm to understand.

Laura:

How long in physical linear time does it take for a soul or spirit to leave the body?

Jill:

This is very individual as well and again it is a freewill choice. There are different realms of dimensions and frequencies. The third dimension is the realm that you have chosen to incarnate in for this lifetime. When the soul leaves the physical body many times what we have witnessed is that soul makes the free will choice to remain in a frequency and vibration closely connected to the third dimension so that they can experience and feel close to their loved ones while their loved ones can feel close to them as well.

For many of you, you may feel your loved ones closer to you for days or weeks after their physical transition and then you may not be able to feel them for a while. Every individual is different so while we cannot put a definitive time and we know you humans like definitive linear days and times we just need to explain that this is very individual.

But what we can say with your linear time the average seems to be from hours to even some choose weeks. That time period, if they have again chosen to completely make their transition to the other realm then they will go into the healing chamber. What we have seen is every individual soul is different depending on the traumas that accompanied the soul from this past incarnation, the time spent in the healing chamber seems to be anywhere from days to months in your linear time.

Laura:

Would it make sense, with a capital S, that the acceptance and love and forgiveness of the loved ones on Earth would play an intimate role in the resolve of the person that has crossed over. Would this make their journey an easier and more seamless one?

Jill:

Absolutely, without doubt. This is one thing that we can confirm that as the energy is connected and we are all connected and while those of us communicating right now are in a higher vibrational realm using the channel known as Jill M Jackson, we are all intricately connected to each other.

If each person can understand that giving forgiveness and understanding and love to their loved one who for whatever reason made the free will choice to end this physical incarnation before their soul contract, this will assist each one of your loved ones on their healing journey.

At the same time, dear ones, it will assist you on your physical journey in this lifetime. So, there is no other way to explain this other than everything is based on higher vibrational frequencies such as love and forgiveness and understanding.

Laura:

Given that we're all connected can you confirm that this also plays a vital role in the imprint and the energetic signature of the unborn children in the future generation?

Jill:

Everything is connected. Everything is absolutely interwoven and connected. What we have witnessed in some souls with their own freewill who have either ended their physical incarnation through what you term, suicide, or through an untimely death may choose to reincarnate in a very quick manner using your linear time space, knowledge from your dimension.

The energy and the frequency are interwoven through the souls, through the unborn children because the energy and the frequency is connected to each soul's signature. Each soul that inhabits each soul group in the other realms is interconnected with each other and their signature.

So, yes, each and every one of these experiences is connected to future incarnations. However, we do need to explain that there are souls choosing to incarnate in this realm from other realms that have not had physical incarnations on this planet.

So, with those situations there will be a connection but not the same intricate connection from the souls who had a physical, familial incarnation on your planet. We understand that this is very complex, and we are attempting to explain this from what those of you in the physical world can understand.

Laura:

The heart knows, yes?

Jill:

The heart knows, yes.

Laura

What would be the term the spirits or the spirit guides would use for suicide?

Jill:

Our terms in the other realms are much different than human terms. We would prefer not putting a human term but the understanding that we have is more of an uncompleted soul contract.

Laura:

For someone who is grieving the loss of a loved one is there a simple practice even for what we would call the nay-sayers that would help them to intimately know that their loved one is not lost? That they're still available for connection?

Jill:

We invite each person to open their awareness and even for those nay-sayers as you say or sceptical minded individuals we would invite you to open your awareness and to practice the frequency of love because when each person and each individual is in the frequency of love this is a vibration that is high enough to be able to feel, see, sense, smell and to hear your loved ones who are always, always communicating and letting you know that they are not lost.

They are simply residing in another world, what we call the other world. We encourage you to open your vibration and to sit in a frequency of love because this awakens your awareness to be able to hear their words and to be able to hear them when they call your name, to be able to smell them, and to be able to sense and know that they are with you, and some of you are even able to see them. Some of you are able to experience them in your dream state.

What we encourage you to do is not go into the negative, nay-sayer, what we call the ego mind, and to say that your experiences with your loved ones are not real because they are. Your loved ones are always with you and your loved ones are always giving you signs that they are with you, always.

They do this through leaving coins, they do this through leaving feathers, they do this through sometimes moving items in your home. Your human mind cannot grasp that this is even possible, but we are here to excitedly to tell you that this is possible. They reside in a higher frequency and so much build up their energetic signature so to speak to be able to lower their frequency to come into your realm, that's why these signs that you are waiting for may not happen as often as you like.

Many of the signs come through the animal kingdom because it's not that your loved ones inhabit the bodies of the animals, of the hawks and the butterflies and the turtles but they have a synchronistic agreement with these animals to be able to help them give these signs and work with them to be able to show you, their loved ones that they are always, always right there.

Laura:

Is the death experience painful?

Jill:

Absolutely not. This is another message that we would love to be able to explain to all of you. The death experience is not painful. For your loved ones who have experienced death through transition, through accidents, while it may seem in the physical realm that this was quite painful, please understand that the soul leaves the physical body and does not experience this pain.

This is something that we really want to get the message out that every loved one that we have communicated with needs their loved ones to know that while it may seem like the human body is experiencing pain through whatever trauma their transition was that their soul has separated from the body.

Laura:

Is there a tunnel of light? If so, what is that?

Jill:

We will try to explain this in human terms but again, every individual has a free will experience, but yes there is what you would call a tunnel of light. The best way that we can explain what this is, is energy and frequency. Those realms that we are residing in depending on each individual's soul would be the fifth dimension or higher dimensions.

The frequency is so fast and vibrating so fast that it manifests in what you would term light. So, yes, it does appear as a tunnel of light. What we can also say is that it is one of the most beautiful experiences, the humans that have had the near-death experiences will be able to explain this as well.

As human channels who have been in this frequency it's so pure and filled with such unconditional love that we want to encourage each one of you not to be frightened when your time comes because each individual will have an experience of transitioning into the other realms, and we want to invite you to understand that this is nothing to fear.

It is a beautiful process with frequency of unconditional love and your loved ones, and your angels and your guides waiting to hand out their hand to assist you in this transition. But we also would like you to understand that while many of you look up to the heavenly realms and the stars, the best way we can explain is the other realm is inches in your terminology from each one of you. It's very, very close in frequency.

Laura:

What is the divine purpose for the year 2020?

Jill:

We are smiling because so many that are incarnated during the year 2020 viewed this as such a challenging year in your calendar. The year 2020 was an opportunity for exponential growth and ascension to the higher realms. This was an opportunity for reflection, for each and every individual incarnated on your planet, this was an opportunity to go within and to be able to witness and see that your soul choose to incarnate during this lifetime not to be on, what you term the rat race. Not to be on, another term you humans use, the hamster wheel.

The purpose of the soul's incarnation is for evolution and growth. The year 2020 was an opportunity for this, not only for each individual and we would like to say that we are pleased with how many of your masses have understood this and how many have utilised this year of 2020 to go within and to understand that everything is about love, and everything is about connection.

We are pleased with the residual mass awakening of so many of you. At the same time we are still witnessing so many in the human realm going into a vibration of fear. We encourage each one of you not to remain in a vibration of fear because we all transition at some point or another.

This experience is not about staying in a vibration of fear, it is about reaching out and connecting. We encourage each one of you not to remain in isolation for long periods of time because the human experience as well as the experience in the other realms is about connection.

Yes, we are so elated that you are able to connect with each other through your World Wide Web and we are excited about this. By the way this is leading you to a more of a telepathic type experience because if you look at the World Wide Web as a way of instant communication so to speak, this is the opportunity for each individual incarnated to be able to understand that you each have this ability within each one of you to connect telepathically. The year 2020 was about this. It was about connection, reflection, introspection, and growth.

Laura:

If I am someone who is in isolation and depression and have been accustomed to a life of fear, and I have quantified my worth and don't really feel worthy of love and connection, what might you say to me to allow me to open up to receive another into my life and to feel love?

Jill:

Our dear ones, everything is a vibration of love, and the year 2021 is about loving yourself more than any other. We invite each one of you to embrace this soul growth opportunity for the year 2021 in your time space continuum to embrace self-love. We invite each one of you to remember that you are sovereign beings. You have freewill.

Each one of you can learn to love yourselves in this way, in the beautiful opportunity that you have on your planet with the invention of the World Wide Web. There is help and assistance everywhere. There are groups, there are people who dedicate this incarnation to helping each individual love themselves more. That is our message for you in 2021.

We encourage you to take baby steps with this. We encourage you to lovingly give yourself time to get to a place to fully love yourselves, but we would like to remind you that each one of you has this capacity within yourselves. We ask you to remember that you are part of source, you are intricately part of creator, you are part of each one of your guides, each one of your angels that is vibrating at least at a frequency of fifth dimension or higher, connect with them, sit in silence and meditation and ask them to blend with you.

Through this blending you will be able to feel this unconditional love. This will help you in your human terms get to a place where it is known, understood. We also ask you to remember that you are experiencing a human realm.

You have chosen to be in the third dimension and part of the third dimensional experience is lower vibrational frequencies and not being in a place of beating yourself up so to speak for having periods of sadness or having periods of loneliness or grieving someone who is not physically connected to you.

But what we invite you to do is remember to do your best, to stay in these vibrational frequencies for shorter periods of time because everything is love. You are love. You are part of us. You are part of the creator and it is impossible, dear ones, to be connected to the creator and not feel love. The moments of not feeling love are human experiences, dear ones, these are temporary human experiences.

Laura:

Is there anything else that you would like to share at this time?

Jill:

We want each one of you to know that you are a diamond in the rough, your choice to incarnate in this third dimensional planet earth was a challenging one, dear ones, because this frequency is dense. So, we would like to lovingly applaud each one of you for having the courage to experience this third dimensional opportunity for soul growth and expansion, so bravo.

We would like to ask you to remember that you are Source. We would lovingly ask you to remember that you are perfect just the way you are, and you are loved just the way you are, and we are here to help each one of you through your challenges and to remind you that you are never alone.

What we invite you to remember is introspection, centeredness, meditation, yoga, these types of connections, also your connection with nature, nature is love. The trees are love. Animals are love. The animals on your planet are incarnated to help each of you know and understand what unconditional love is.

Embrace your animal kingdom, embrace your plant and your trees, and the wind, and the sun, and the moon because when you connect with these energies it will be much easier for you to experience love and to stay in a vibration of love. That is all.

Jill is an international award winning highly sought after Psychic Medium and Spiritual Teacher having won such prestigious awards such as the 2016 and 2015 Psychic of the Year from Best American Psychics!

https://jillmjackson.com/

WINGING IT WITH JAN SALERNO AND THE GODDESS COUNCIL

Laura:

If someone was on the verge of ending their life, feeling not the fabric of their identity and their experience had been ripped away. What words, what wisdom, what reminders would want to be shared to activate a remembrance within this being?

Jan:

Remember, the Truth of who you are. Come to your center. Allow any misconstructions...the definitions, the overlays, the hurts and the presumptions that the mind in turmoil can make, to dissolve.

Use a sword of light, call upon Creator, call upon your Creator, call upon your 'I Am Presence' and stand in your space where you are and with your breath, breathe in presence and strength to fill your body and your field.

Releasing, with the out-breath, that which is not true, that which you are not. Breathing in, illuminating, breathing in the light, and the presence of who you are, breathing out what you are not. Simply going to the breath.

The mind can determine so much through distortion when the mind is not clear, empty, and remember that you are love, a breathing being of love and light on this planet.

Find your center first and foremost.

As I draw from the twelve images of the Goddess Council and Adiamanta comes through. She is a multidimensional being, spanning dimensions and timelines seeking joy and compassion. If you are experiencing turmoil and a sense of being and are on the precipice, go inside each and every room inside your house - the house in your mind, into your brain, your consciousness. Go to each and every construct you've created or determined and bring compassion here.

You begin doing some housekeeping, sweeping up the corners, bringing light to that room if you feel a darkness in there. Go into Ho'oponopono that's a Hawaiian forgiveness chant, a forgiveness practice. You're going within and you're calling, "I love you. I'm sorry. Please forgive me. Thank you."

When you go into these 'rooms' within yourself you can feel a blip or bump, or where you're caught. Bring forgiveness and release to that place. Scan your consciousness completely over and over again. Do it the next day and the next day to relieve the hold that your mind has determined with. Free yourself from the pattern and cycle.

The heart, the healed heart, in an ideal world would rule as opposed to the mind and the constructs that we can create. Bring compassion to yourself and each and every one on the planet. Everyone is walking their path through the minefield of distortions and beauty and what we feel this means about us.

Somebody turns their head, or somebody says a non-encouraging word or worse, what have we determined that means about us? This is where the pain is and let it go. I love you. I'm sorry. Please forgive me, you're forgiving yourself, and thank you for the lesson. You will get better and better and better. It will be easier and easier, taking little bites out of that.

The image I have is sitting on the shore of a dark lake. Our hand is touching the water of this dark lake. We can use our instrument, our physical instrument, to bring light through our Will down through our head, down into our throat, down, down, into our heart and we can clear the water of our consciousness with touch by putting our hand in the water through our imagination, our inner vision.

We're 75% water. The planet is 75% water. We can, with a prayer of beauty and love, bring that beauty and love, the presence within our bodies, within this dark lake that we've created.

It's a choice. We're in choice. We're beings of free choice. Bring that love that we're not feeling from outside of yourself and bring it to yourself.

Be your own best loving parent, who in an ideal life you could imagine would have been there all along, loving you, supporting you, recognising your innocence, your tenderness and sensitivity, your strengths and who wouldn't turn away.

Who would be there all the time. You have those ideal inner parents within yourself, aspects of yourself, so parent yourself, bring that to you here.

Tell yourself, "You can do this." Listen to the words of your ideal parents within you and if they are not good words that you hear yourself saying, and it is something that is dark or isn't really the truth of you, let that go.

If you are using self-talk that beats you down, you have to stop and look at that.

"Why are you beating yourself up?" That's a loop that you're in and you've got to take control of this mind like wild stallions, tame it. Like the yogis in India have done, tame that wild mind.

If it wants to keep going, change the script. Be the beautiful parents, loving you, seeing you, your beloved, recognising your heart and encouraging you to come forth, because you are in there.

You are a beautiful, loving, kind, strong, true light, who you truly are and born into this body is here. Get to know yourself.

Laura:

If the pain is too much, if the discomfort is too much to remain in the body, and someone chooses to end their life, what happens on the other side?

Jan:

We live in a compassionate multiverse. We're on our journey home where we take a body, this body, to evolve the soul. We polish the facets of our unique diamond of our presence day to day. There is much love in the multiverse to receive us home.

Living on this beautiful Earth has many constructs within it. There is so much to experience on this planet. I would say if somebody is feeling that close to wanting to stop the ability to make choices, buy a one-way ticket somewhere.

Your problems will eventually follow you or find you but you can get a break from the pattern and something needs to die and maybe many things need to die but leave your body out of it.

Get some room in the field that you're in. If you are having a very difficult time clearing that field... just ask for help. Help is all around us. I mean help within, calling upon your Creator, your Higher Self, beyond any religion or spiritual construct that you may have grown up in and rejected, but to that Divine Intelligence that breathes your body and that beats your heart, that causes you to grow from a baby into an adult.

That Divine Intelligence is within you and is your operating system. It's in each and every cell of your body. So, there's some intelligence there to access and if your life, as such, or your choices have brought you to a place of such total darkness, buy a ticket, get out. Walk out of there. Just keep going. Get some room.

Ask for Divine assistance. Ask for the truth of who you are. Ask for the next step. Breathe, presence where you are. Ask what's the next step? Make a step forward.

I've a dear friend who's daughter committed suicide. She found her in the basement. The daughter was 14 years old, and had been battling with her mom at the time, as teens can.

Her momma was beyond devastated. She came to me 10 years later in deep grief and looking ancient, and was ready to release the grief. She couldn't carry the weight anymore. It was too big.

She didn't want to go the path of her daughter, but she didn't know what to do, but she knew she was ready to end this grief.

She reached out to her friends and several of those friends were in a seminar together with me. We took her to a particular sacred beach here in Hawaii and did a release ceremony.

We had a golden chord, carpenter's string and binding and we wrapped this heavy rock which represented the grief.

We gave her a very dull paring knife and we let her tie herself up with this string and hold the rock. We were all surrounding her, and took her out to the deeper water. When she was ready, we moved away, still encircling her, so she could feel the weight of her grief.

She had to struggle to cut herself free. She made a very physical effort, as we all held space for her as she physically made a statement to cut herself free from the grief.

She was ready to feel the weight of that go, and that acting out and being supported and witnessed in doing so, was so powerful.

She had a magical release and she felt so much better. Four years later I saw her, she had developed a book and had just published it. She had begun to hear her daughter speak to her, made the connection and wrote this book from her daughters' perspective of crossing over day by day. The book also included my friend's accounting of her own journey for weeks, months and years after her daughters suicide. One chapter the daughter's, the next the mother's and so on.

I have a very vivid visual of what this girl experienced passing through to the other side. On the other side it was the same girl, same attitude, growing up through her attitude. She was still where she was in her growth, emotional growth, and she grew, and she grew, and she grew. She was guided throughout and then began to help people who had passed through in the same way, a similar way on her own.

Profound wisdom and assurance has come from that book and continues to come through to the mother who wrote the book. Now she's found her daughter and they have a very, very strong daily connection and communication.

We can think we're very alone but it's our mind. It's our own construct. It's our own punishing of ourselves. We're not seeing who we truly are and thinking that our creator would punish us or allow us to be alone when this is not at all the case.

It's like sitting in front of a banquet table and starving to death. Ask for help. Help us everywhere, and each one of the faces that we see around us. We have eight billion faces to choose from, to be just the help we need. Ask and you shall receive.

My meditations have shown me to ask, to ask the question, how can we get answers if we don't ask, how we starve if we don't eat from the banquet table of life. There is help.

Addiction and toxic relationships, toxic thoughts, whatever is not working, you can slide out. Just choose, choose. Then you become good at it.

Make the choice, make the choice again, make the choice again, make the choice again. Breathe, get bigger, make the choice again. Breathe, get bigger, remember with the out-breath to let go of what's not working.

I have drawn another card from the Goddess Council, I get Osirene - transmute, transmute, transmute. She's working the violet flame of transmutation here. The truth of who we are, we have angels and guides and helpers who are holding that place of truth and transmutation for us and for the planet for all time.

Laura:

For those that have ended their lives, is there an energetic signature, or a continued process when we leave the physical body, when they return to Source?

Jan:

L'ea came to that, from the heart and these ever waves of loving. When we forget love, if we forget that we are loved, if we forget that we are loving beings we take our life and decide to check out.

We try to hold in our limited capacity of a mind, a limited construct, we're making our Creator or the hierarchy as we imagine it and all that, we can make it very small and we can make it punishing, and we can make it like it's holding us back when our journey is our journey and it's perfect.

Cultures in the past found the conscious choosing of an ending of their life acceptable within the confines of their cultural attitudes.

It's the journey that we're choosing. As beings of free choice we have probably all chosen to check out at some point prematurely before the end of our life. Some people get big diseases, is that not a choice on some level, to check out with that? I get that sometimes we've kind of painted ourselves into a corner with our beliefs and some people can be free while they're alive and some people's beliefs are so strong. As an example, deep religious beliefs - that you have to do this, and you have to do that, and it has to be like this.

It's very hard to live in a society where everything is so small and rigid. I've got to be rigid...my kids don't do that and they're gone and I'm all alone and... and... But, if you don't allow some room in those beliefs, it would be sad and small maybe you would check out at some point through a major illness or something like that so then you can be free to release that mind construct That mind construct is the part of us, our self-imposed acceptance or creation of a mind construct that says my only choice or that my best choice is to check out, take my life rather than greet the new day.

What does today have to bring? Even if it's not optimal or it's been of your making. We forget that we're powerful creators, we're not broken. We're creating something in a limited way, to expand our palate,and be creative. It's like if I just painted or drew with a pencil, I can't make my world technicolour. My life is black and white, and grey. Use colour!

If you find your life is black and grey, expand your palate and tools in your creation, take a class that is stretching you in a direction you haven't stretched before, just to stretch your mind, to remember how to learn and to stretch. You might not take that skillset that you're learning into the future, but you will get something out of it because you're breaking patterns and breaking habits.

When we are so attached, we hold on so deeply to our beliefs, we want to be right...therefore if I believe nobody loves me or if I believe I'm ugly, whatever it is I believe, we are going to look through the lens of those beliefs.

"Did you hear what that guy said?" Or that person "See, they think I'm ugly. They don't accept me so I'm not going to accept me." That's what that means. we determine what we think that means about us, our beliefs colour our reality and we're going to make sure we're such perfect creators. We're creators in the making and we're perfect creators.

We are going to make that mean that if I believe I'm ugly I'm going to make sure that everybody's reflection back to me supports my belief. You got to look through your life with that because it's profound, it's true. So, this part,this mind here, this mind...well we want to lead with the heart, and we need help here.

What are we thinking? Self-reflect, what are you telling yourself about yourself? What do you believe? Why do you believe that? When did you start that belief? Go through and weed your mind methodically. The first thing I believed was when I was three years old, and I think that was meant about me."

Well, does that still mean that now? "Well..." So, you can weed that one and if there's ones you still don't know about, leave them in a pile just suspend belief even for a month. Put those, "Well I don't know if those beliefs are true but I'm going to put them in a pile." You can always pick them up a month later and believe them again, but you would get a lot of room, and breathe into that room for the possibility.

Every culture and person, has beliefs about themselves or beliefs about the world. Some of them are true, and some of them aren't. It's important to check in, what am I believing in? Why do I believe I don't have any other choice and that my best choice is to check out?

We can have a thought that will produce a feeling. It happens in an instant. If we think that thought, one, two, three more times, now we're feeling our blood pressure just went up, we're feeling sad, we're feeling compressed, all these things and we did it with our belief... our thought.

This is where we need to free our minds, flush out things that aren't true, what are you telling yourself? Spend your time looking within.

Turn off the tv, and go inside and do some inner housekeeping. If you did that as a practice, five minutes a day, you're going to get some room in there from niggly beliefs you didn't even notice like I can't do that, I'm getting too old, whatever it is you know.

Laura:

Is there any shame or disappointment coming from the ancestors towards anyone who has taken their own life?

Jan:

In my heart of hearts I don't think so, what I get is a welcoming home, and any and everyone our ancestors or people who have done an earth walk know the challenges.

If we were born into complete slavery in chains and then passed away because we were murdered or starved, we are going to be received by the ocean of humanity that is just a dimension away. We are not our bodies. Our soul in our presents goes on. We are not in a punishing multiverse.

The Creator has bigger plans for us than to shame us. Like a parent and a child. I wouldn't bring a child in to completely shame them or shoot them in the foot and mock every mistake, because they weren't strong, or if they didn't know how to do something, to mock them for not doing it.

The earth walk is not easy. Each one of our challenges it's like a pearl, the sand and the oyster. We create a pearl... Lessons learned. Each one of these life lessons we have all had – really rough ones, easier ones, times of beauty for a short time or a long time, or chapters.

If you're not liking the chapter you're living or writing about, you might want to reflect on what it is that you are learning here? What are you getting out of this? Am I done? Have I just drained this dry? Is there nothing left here?

You have a chance to check in and if you're creating negativity around you, you can change it up.

I know some religions find it a sin, or sinful, or horrific, if you take your life.

I believe we are dealt with by our team on the other side in love and light. If we OD'd, we were on a path that we didn't change and that is an unfortunate situation or blip in the radar on that path.

What can we do about this on the other side?

We missed an opportunity, maybe then we missed having our children and missed having a wife or husband where we got to really help the planet, or I know many people in my older life who had OD'd by going into 'recreational' drugs.

I don't think that if someone is chemically depressed when they pass through to the other side, that they will be held down because they were so depressed. It's like that's a chemical imbalance and they didn't find the chemistry or the help.

Why are we going to believe the lesser version about ourselves as opposed to believing the biggest, beautiful dream about ourselves?

If we are such grand creators, I mean you look at the Da Vinci and the Mozart and the amazing singers and painters and dancers and all these people that are on the planet, are we going to believe that we are a small one rather than that we have the potential to be anything we want but it's making that choice. You know? And giving yourself good guidance and good accolades on the way and then getting a team of mentors.

If your parents and the people around you aren't ideal for you, get a one-way ticket out of Dodge and go someplace else and get yourself involved in the community, find people. Find people, there are people everywhere who are helping other people. It's an incredible gift to help somebody else. It's an incredible gift to be of assistance. You realize that a powerful, positive reflection will give you a lot of room to grow, give yourself that positive reflection.We are infinite beings... as we are eternal, think big. Dream big.

Jan:

This book, The Dreaming Road by Betty Moore is the book I shared earlier. Her daughter is on the other side helping people, she was embraced in a school on that other side.

The school is about helping people who have passed over. There are many near death experiences that people have shared that you can find on the internet. Thomas Mellon Benedict is an amazing story that this gentleman shared. I think that it's not just one way.

We can create hell, if you want to be in hell and you want to create hell when you passover, I think you have a choice to create that for a while but then I think that will run out because we're still beings of free choice so let the light in, let the light in.

Laura:

Is there an aspect of our personality, memories, identity that is brought through the veil when we return "home"?

Jan:

I have experienced people who have passed through my dreams. When I dreamt of my father who had passed and my first husband who had passed, I saw and heard "them". This may be my identification with them, but I can see that they carry some remembrance of what they went through.

I think that we're not scrubbed clean of our life. It's said that we get to do a life review. What did we learn? What didn't we learn? This dreaming world story I told you, where this child was a 14-year-old when she passed over. Sassy, sneaky, pouty and she worked through that.

Years of growth on the other side. She is about 29 now. My friend has a relationship with her as a 29-year-old as opposed to that same 14-year-old.

The Dalai Lama said that everyone has been your child, you're mother, father, lover, husband, aunt, uncle, child, you've been my son, you've been my daughter, you've been my worst enemy,and my greatest friend.

So, a school of thought is we've all gone through so many incarnations, supposedly, according to the Dalai Lama and Buddhist thought that we have been all these things to each other, all these relationships. Each relationship polishes us and polishes us. We've been on a wheel of death and rebirth.

In the multiverse, I think that our construct is too small, but we are evolving. We come here to evolve. We get better. We at times make mistakes, but we continue to get better. We are evolving better and better and better to reflect on each other and to become more empowered, to release attachment and to love, bigger, better and with more open hearts.

I think that we probably pass over with some memories. When my dad passed, I was standing at the head of the bed, as he was getting cold on the bed. I was holding him in the hospital and I was seeing myself and him at the head of the bed.

I was holding darshan for my dad and he was in this swashbuckling shirt looking at me, looking at his body there, multidimensionally. I was there at his side.

The expression on his face as he was standing there looking at his body, and the relationship and the everything that he had been to everything was one of total disbelief, shock. It seemed as though he was realizing a bit of what he had done. Wondering what was going on? I think we have a period of time of transition.

I recently did a family constellation and my dad was in it. I did some more healing and freeing for him so that he didn't carry to the other side so much of his belief that he was a bad man and had screwed things up here in his life.

I have been told in my prayers, that we hold the power to heal each other's karma. If I want to punish my dad for this life, I guess I could because of his mistakes but I can choose not to as well. I can release him and myself from that darkness and just love him, and recognise that we're all imperfect, stepping into our power as creators. We're beings of free choice.

Jan:

I would like to draw one more card, for one last message. ARCTUR came through. She's about crystal technologies. She is like The Science Officer. The message is that everything is so much bigger than we can really imagine.

We're so big we can create worlds and we're just on our way. Like a hive of bees, they all go back every night to the hive, the first ones get there first, and the last ones get there last, but the whole hive of bees goes back every night to their hive. We're staggered, we can't all fit through the whole at the same time. Move over.

Laura:

I was feeling that as we are trying to wrap our heads around what goes on 'out there', it feels to me that it is literally not something that can be known but is felt. It's hard to even begin to talk about it. My psyche gets blasted if it tries to comprehend, however my body and my being knows it.

Jan:

The heart will heal if we breathe in and release our attachments. We are so good at creating. We can create rooms in the mind, we can create all of these constructs and the image around ARCTUR's head is showing all of these facets and constructs.

Imagine if your head was in the middle of a big giant quartz crystal, absolutely pure, or a diamond and just polishing everything and clearing out any debris. We don't even have to think of what it is specifically, we can just ask for help to clear it out. Our job is to take the trash out.

Laura:

Yes, we need to flush the mental toilet.

The Goddess Council ...a counsel of starlight that came to and through Jan, with grace. Initially as 12 light beings, loving voices from the multiverse in response to my crying for a vision in image and word. How and why was I spared in the tsunami of 2004? This Counsel of starlight continues to sprinkle wisdom and inspiration on how to navigate this life in the most joyous ways.

Contact:

Jan and/or to work intimately with THE GODDESS COUNCIL Deck:

thegoddesscouncil.com

WINGING IT WITH LORCAN O'TOOLE

Laura:

If you had words of wisdom to share with someone who is ready to take their own life, what is it you would want them to know and to remember?

Lorcan:

First and foremost, you may not think you know who I am, but I love you because I am you.

Laura:

Am I a bad person for wanting to end my life?

Lorcan:

For centuries if not millennia, people, human beings, humans have experienced an echo chamber of what we would refer to as judgement. Judgment not as in discernment but condemnation, say the ugly side of judgement, of condemning, of referring to something as bad, as not good enough, as insufficient, not worthy of love. We've heard these echo chambers through our parents, through our schools, through our friends, through our loved ones, through our media, through our television, films. Continuing this cycle of judgement, of evaluation.

If you look at nature, you look at the flowers, you look at the trees, you look at the birds, and the seas, and the oceans, you don't see another tree or another flower saying that the other one is not good enough or judging or evaluating the worthiness of any other part of one blade of grass or one other tree or flower.

It exists as a harmonious universal song of love, of unity and yet the human beings have learned, taken on board, this mental cerebral evaluation of ourselves and each other as imperfect or good or bad or less than. Many of us being very sensitive have taken into our hearts, into our souls, into our mind the idea that unless you do enough homework, unless you work very hard, unless you work yourself into the ground, quite literally in some circumstances, that you're not good enough.

This is an overwhelming degree of pressure that is unnecessary, fundamentally is an illusion and yet it feels very real to us and it feels not only real, it feels very heavy, it feels very dense, it feels overwhelming like we're carrying a massive burning boulder and that if we don't carry that massive boulder that somehow, we're letting ourselves down.

So, for a little boy or a little girl to go to its mother or it's father and say, "Hello Mommy, hello Daddy. Am I doing a good job?" And they're told, "No it's not good enough. You need to stop looking out the window. You need to concentrate on calculus." Then the little boy or little girl feels dismayed, all it wanted was loving, open, kind communication and the response to that need or however you want to put it is a cold, mental, evaluative judgement, devoid of emotion, devoid of heart and the effect that that has as the little boy or little girl takes on board that energy and believes because we are fundamentally loving beings of light and illumination it takes on board that suggestion that somehow love is connected to judgement and that's part of what love is.

So, if we say that's good, or that's bad, or you swipe right, or your swipe left that somehow that's to do with unconditional love. We take that onboard so much that it becomes part of our evaluative experience of life and each other. Again, looking at the flowers, and the trees and the plants and the birds they're existing as a unity, as a oneness, as a community, as a song, a harmonious song, millions of different instruments playing together and yet the dissonance of what we experience as human beings as judgement stops the song, takes the record off the needle, the needle off the record. It's abrupt.

It's so abrupt that our hearts shut down and when we're feeling our hearts open, we feel connection to each other, we feel a connection to all of life, to all of the human family. When this energy of judgement comes in our hearts shut down, we close off our communication with our divinity, with our heart and what that causes is a void, a feeling of abandonment, a feeling or rejection, a feeling of not belonging.

Somehow that's because we're disconnected from our feelings, from our hearts, from our love, that we're not worthy of experiencing it. Then, we get into our minds and our minds start to takeover and start to go on a crusade, a campaign of attempting to prove our worthiness, attempting to prove that we're lovable. We knock ourselves out, we push ourselves, we carry the boulder of shame and guilt and lament to such a degree that it becomes our lives, and we forget that we're the flowers, and the trees in the breeze.

Everything becomes heavy and dense, and it becomes overwhelming because it's not supposed to be, the light that you are, the consciousness that you are, the divinity that you are is an energy of warmth, of care, of compassion of unending support and kindness, that is the essence of the universal oneness. Which is why it's so painful for us to experience the idea of being separated from that kindness and warmth and care because the reason it feels painful, the reason the boulder feels so heavy is because it's not true.

The illusion feels real, but you can tell it's an illusion when you feel despair, when you feel overwhelmed, when you feel the weight of the world on your shoulders. What that is, is life indicating to you that that's not the case, it's not the case at all. It's a signpost nudging you back, signing a song to remind you of your truth, of the clarity of what you know to be true of yourself and of life. As this light, as this warmth-ness, kindness we've taken on board so many different codes and programs and ideas from reality, from our parents and otherwise that has convinced us in a mental and cerebral way that we're disconnected, that we're separated, that we're unworthy of the truth of who we are.

So, if you find yourself thinking of the idea of taking your own life, take a step back in the lens, breathe and ask your heart, "Remind me of what it feels like to be who I am." There are so many painful experiences in life, and yet all of them that we experience, regardless of what they are in their nature, all have a purpose. It seems challenging to realise that in the face of the painful experiences and the challenges however you want to label them but every single loss, every single death, every single heartbreak, every single rejection encased, encroached, ingrained within every single one of those experiences is an enormously positive opportunity.

It just depends on how you're wishing to perceive those experiences. You can see it as that you are a victim and that life is awful and then you die and it's a miserable experience, or you can refrain and see that within every single one of those experiences, in all of that darkness, within the depths of that darkness is the brightest light you could ever imagine. Life is not cruel, it is not a judge, and a jury, and a police officer. It is like the most caring, loving mother, and father, and teacher you could ever imagine, offering you experiences that potentially can nudge you into loving your life and loving life more than you could ever have thought that you could.

If you go to apply for a job and you get turned down, maybe ask yourself did you really want that job? Or, where you trying to get that job to prove to yourself or someone else that you are worthy of love? Maybe you didn't get the job because life had something different to offer you. Or, if you met a nice guy or a nice girl and they turned you down. You can either say, "Well I got turned down because I'm not good enough." Or because life again was guiding you to something else that was more of a match for you.

Or, even a Coronavirus epidemic, you could say, "Well, oh my goodness, the whole world's gone to pot. Everything's terrible, disconnected." And all this, but actually within the Corona experience there's been one of the most profound opportunities human beings have ever had to go within themselves, to disconnect from the ridiculously fast paced consumeristic, journey of the earth, it's been wreaking havoc upon the earth and destroying the forest, an opportunity to connect with ourselves, with our emotions, with our hearts to take a breath, to take time, to be with ourselves, to learn who we are.

You say, "My goodness. Thank you so much Coronavirus. You were sent by the divinity to give all of us a profound opportunity." With a death of a loved one, a mother or a father, can say - one second - how is that an opportunity? I loved that person very dearly and now they're gone, and I cannot hug them anymore, and I cannot speak with them anymore. How on earth could that be an opportunity?

The thing about the opportunity is that we all carry within ourselves as souls from many incarnations, from many experiences of life, tremendous amount of grief, of pain, of trauma, and sometimes when you lose a loved one or something seemingly goes wrong in your life, what this does is awaken this wound, these wounds that are within ourselves and gives it an opportunity to come out, to be expressed and also chiefly, that when you're in your heart, when you're connected to all of spirit and then a judgement comes along and then you feel cut off from that, that opportunity to have a loved one physically who dies and then experience finding that love and that connection within yourself is one of the most satisfying, empowering, connecting beautiful and surprising experiences that you could have.

That this person that's gone was the one that loved me, but then you can find that love for yourself within yourself. One day you might end up thanking the person that you think you lost because they gave you an opportunity to find that within yourself for that what you were looking outside of yourself for.

Many times the idea of suicide and killing oneself arises because there is so much going in the heart, so many emotions, so many feelings, so much pain and sometimes so much beauty and joy that it becomes overwhelming and that we go into a form of denial about it. One of the first thing that the mind goes to is, "I want to kill myself." My partner broke up with me I want to kill myself. I don't have any money. I want to kill myself. I lost my job I want to kill myself.

One of the reasons this occurs is because we have so much going on within ourselves that it's easier sometimes to come up with the idea of killing ourselves because we would be able to put all of that underneath the rug and not have to process it, not have to feel it especially and that we'd do anything to not feel our feelings. It takes courage, it takes surrender, it takes compassion on a very deep and tender level within yourself to go into your feelings, to explore them, to experience them, which many times is accompanied by floods of tears, songs of pain, many times when people cry the most, they laugh.

At the same time when people laugh the most, they cry. The mind comes up with 144,000 different excuses not to feel but if you feel, if you feel the love, the presence within yourself and within everything many times you've stopped thinking about yourself so much. The first thing you want to do is to be of assistance to everyone and everything else. One of the most powerful ways to go through the experience of the pain that we carry is to see another person who is in more pain than you are and immediately you stop thinking so much about yourself and a level of compassion and care overwhelms you in a beautiful way, of saying, "My goodness. This person is in a lot more pain than I am. I want to put an arm around them. I would like to remind them that they're loved, remind them who they are, and be of assistance in some way."

What that does is shows us a mirror of how we could be kinder to ourselves. I need more compassion, I need to be more compassionate with myself, it would be more beautiful to be more gentle with myself, be more nurturing to myself. I can show it to someone else so if I'm showing it to someone else then I can show it to myself. Also, there are people who have taken their own lives and are taking their lives and will take their own lives so to speak. From the spiritual perspective there is absolutely no judgement around that. There is no hell or fiery consequences or retributions, only loving consideration.

The irony of that statement is that it is the energy of judgement itself which is behind all of the suffering, and all of the ideas of suicide and rejection and abandonment that humans feel behind all of it. So, quite simply, to move into your heart into an all-inclusive compassionate, conscious, experience of yourself and of all of life and every human being that walks the earth, is a frequency where the idea of judgment does not exist. You are loved, you are love, you are loving and that is all and that is everything.

Laura:

What is spirit's interpretation of the original sin?

Lorcan:

The idea of sin is an illusion, it doesn't exist. Sin is a judgement. Yes, there is wisdom in discerning degrees of sloth, envy, lust, etcetera, etcetera,

etcetera that's going on within you and without you. But, the idea of sin is very much connected to the idea of judgement, to the idea of guilt, to the idea of shame, the idea of carrying a burden.

The original illusion, the original sin, however you wish to frame it is connected to the idea that our true experience is of yourself and when I say self, I don't mean me or a personality. When I say self, I'm talking about everything and everyone, for all of us are the same being looking through different eyes at ourselves, through each other.

The idea that anything is separate from anything else is a mental construct. For the truth, in terms of quantum mechanics and energetic science, is that there is no separation between everything because everything is made up of the same energy, the same consciousness. It is pervasive, absolutely infinite, and there is nothing in creation that is not made of that same conscious intelligence.

The illusion, the original sin comes from the mental construct of the idea that somehow we are separated from our own hearts, separated from divinity, from God, from community, however you wish to frame it which is why when we go through a break up from a loved one we feel the pain and I would say the illusion experienced as pain of separation. It reminds us of many experiences we've had where we have been as our whole selves as we always remain.

We have had incarnations, experiences and many different iterations of for example, coming to earth, stepping down our electromagnetic resonance to a point where we have amnesia, where we can't remember our connection, we can't remember who we are and all considerations and experiences of ourselves.

This is a beautiful mirror of being as divinity as the centre of the heart of all of God's creation and then feeling that we're outside of that and the judgement that we put on ourselves cements, pun intended in terms of the density, cements this feeling of unworthiness, of separation, of rejection, of somehow needing to prove or work ourselves back into heaven, when the truth is that we already are heaven.

We've just come up with this idea which is very painful that we are not. The reason it's painful is to show us the illusory nature of that idea to begin with.

Many times in life we feel contractions, we feel fears, the contractions, the fears are you could say almost the opposite of expansion, of freedom, of openness. Those contractions are an indicator or a signpost of the illusory nature of them to begin with.

We can stub our toe, we can have accidents, we can feel physical pain but emotional pain many times is the resistance to what is good, to what is beautiful, to what is on our side, to what is an opportunity, to what is love which is everything.

The contraction comes from disbelieving that truth to begin with, so the original sin is the illusion that we are separate from our own hearts. That is not a feeling that the heart has, that is the mind, which is why the only journey there is, is from the mind to your very own heart and then back to heaven.

Laura:

What is the divine purpose of the mind?

Lorcan:

Very complex question. The mind in many senses is a tool, and I say this with a lot of care and with a lot of love that you would have for your piano for example, like you would have for your saxophone, "I love you, my piano. I love my saxophone. I even love you my mobile phone." As many people do these days, they seem to have a lot more love for their mobile phones than they do for their very own hearts sometimes.

The mind is a receiving device, its job, its allocation is to be a brilliant and magnificent communication device. It is not intended to invent, it's not intended to come up with things, it is not intended or built to be a creator. It is a medium in which the creator and the universal conscious intelligence to channel through. We are this conscious intelligence. We have convinced ourselves that we have become our minds and that we are our minds.

So much so, that we feel threatened by the idea of severing our mental activity because if we ceased our mental activity we're not going to be able to be worthy, to be able to survive, to be able to function in life, on earth our minds as human beings has been programmed for many thousands of years into a form of survival mode that so much of our mental activity is focused on the idea of putting out fires, of solving problems, of making sure that we have food on our tables, that we have roofs over our head.

The identification that we've brought into as our minds, as opposed to the fullness of the consciousness that we are and the heart that we are has created a situation of dominance and control where the mind attempts to dominant and control our situation, almost like a battle in our day-to-day lives because through that identification and giving that artificial concept of ourselves which people refer to as their personality, free reign to take over driving the car.

Almost like if you had a Range Rover and you gave your seven-year-old child who'd never driven before and said, "Here, get into the driver's seat and drive the car." The little child might be excited at first but then become terrified and overwhelmed with the responsibility of doing something that it's not ready to do.

Our minds are like little children like infants, beautiful, magical, wonderful, precious and special. Yet, like a little child that's told it needs to do it's taxes and drive the Range Rover and look after the entire family and put bread on the table because it's not created by life to be the one driving the car, it gets tremendously overwhelmed and judges itself and feels ashamed and feels unworthy, quite understandably and then it retreats into itself and shuts down and goes into a small little cabinet in the dark and says I don't want to come out because this is too much for me.

This is a beautiful opportunity of transcendence that many are people are going through on the earth right now, they're awakening experience of moving into their sensing and into their feeling senses and experiencing the truth of themselves as consciousness, as the universal heart which is truly the energy driving the car so to speak so that the mind and the inner child does not need to do that anymore it can go and run in the fields and pick a flower and make a sandcastle and relax and not to be the breadwinner of the family.

One of the most beautiful things that was said to me in terms of the mind's understanding of reality, "You don't need to take care of yourself. You are being taken care of and that is you taking care of yourself."

Laura:

Are you saying that I can build sandcastles and money will come?

Lorcan:

This is directly aimed at the inner child because the inner child which many people can also refer to as the mind or the ego is who they have become identified with, and so the consciousness would never ask this question to begin with, but the mind would, the inner child would.

So, I would say to the inner child, "If I build sandcastles, will the money come?" I say the money will come much more smoothly than you ever could have imagined, just like the consistency of the sea and the tides.

You know why? Because you're going to relax. You're going to play. You're going to have fun. You're not going to put so much pressure on yourself. You're going to create a beautiful sandcastle on the glittering sand, watched over by your mummy and daddy and all of consciousness.

In that relaxation in that taking that pressure of your shoulders that's going to open your heart and open your spirit, open up all of your reality and all of your life because you're playing.

The mind has been trained to survive. If I do a job that I don't want to do, and I have no real connection in my heart to it, that will put money on the table, it will put bread on the table, it will put a roof over my head and will ensure my survival. However the consciousness that you are, which is also very much like a playful child, is having a wonderful time just as it is.

Just experiencing the is-ness of the present moment, of the play of love and life, and a smile comes on your face and your nervous system relaxes and your mind goes quiet. Then, your heart opens. That frequency sends out a message to all of creation to reflect back to you the very same energy.

It is my understanding that all of us as individuals, as souls, as human beings have been given a gift or given a gift to ourselves (however you wish to see it) of activities, creativity, wisdom, knowledge, aptitude of particular areas of life which some people could call work, could call hobbies, could call passions.

These gifts come with a hallmark and that hallmark is we love to do them.

Not only just love but we are thrilled to do these things, that are our gifts. You can know that if you are listening to and expressing the gift that you've been given is that it thrills your heart.

You wake up every morning with great joy,excitement and exuberance to employ this gift. The beauty of this gift is that these are gifts that are given to us to give back to everyone else. That's what makes the world go round.

Laura:

Are there any parents on the other side that have messages to share regarding quantifying the worth of their sons and/or daughters?

Lorcan:

Many times sons and daughters of fathers and mothers can and do experience levels of judgement and evaluation from their parents during their lives.

When these mothers and fathers transition to spirit side, first and foremost those levels of judgement dissolve in most cases almost immediately and they also go through a process of seeing their own lives, their own childhood, their own experiences of life that garnishes and flourishes their unconditional compassionate and respect to even more profound levels of expansion because of seeing the pain that others caused them, and the pain they caused to others, and seeing the grand orchestra and purpose of all of it.

For those who have lost a father, who are still alive on the earth, the irony is that they wonder often if they believe in such things, if they're mother or their father is still judging them, is still wagging their finger, and complaining. The irony is that the answer to that question is 99% of the time absolutely no, they're not.

The only one who is judging you is you, because you're still carrying that judgement which you agreed to. For example if someone says you are a bad little boy and you think about it for a moment, you're like "That doesn't feel very good, but my father said it and he loves me so perhaps I am a bad little boy." You agree to that judgement, and then you make a harmony if you want to put that word with that judgement, you match the frequency of it and then you go into what's called self-judgement and the only one that can absolve you of that judgement.

It's not your father or mother in spirit side or even a perceived God, it's you by coming to terms with and accepting and allowing yourself to be the perfection that you are, that you were, and that you always will be. The beauty and the sovereignty of that is in your hands, it is in your hearts and no where else.

Laura:

Is there anything else you would like to share?

Lorcan:

You might not think you know how I am, but what I want to say to you is I'm very proud of you for all that you are experiencing. Remember that even if you're not loving yourself all of life is still loving you constantly, consistently and always. You might believe in your mind that that is not true but to gently, softly, beautifully and gracefully dive into the warm, deep pool, deep lake or ocean of your own heart it will no longer be a question of belief. It will be something that you know.

Lorcan O'Toole is a film-maker, writer, musician, alchemist and spirit-medium.

For more info:

www.unitystar.one

WINGING IT WITH NIGIL MCFARLAND

Laura:

What would you share with someone who feels that the fabric of their lives has been ripped apart?

Nigil:

I think a large majority of the world has gone through a shake up, a heart ache and disorientation. To respond to that I feel what's required, what I have seen in my work and in the work of the people I really enjoy and how they help other people. How do we start to re-engage with life?

What does that mean, really? It means in my opinion it's about coming together and sharing your pain, really allowing to birth this belief that you don't have to be alone with it. Leaning into smaller groups of people, reliable and responsive communities where people look out for you. They hold space. They allow presence, they allow a place for you to not have to alter your state and through disorientation, through the discombobulation, and through the heart pain.

When that's grounded in that there's somebody there that you can lean on and it can help create something new that wasn't there before. Whether it's a new shaping of the mind, an expansion of the heart, a deeper sense of self.

For the hurting individual to move into spaces and places, smaller communities, or groups that's responsive and reliable and in an ordinary way we can get the support of others to move through the pains that we carry and not collapse on them or collapse in on them and allow this just to be a part of a continuation where we grow through the suffering and we don't have to be alone with the pain.

Laura:

What would you say if someone didn't feel worthy of connection or support from others?

Nigil:

Well, let me put this in context. One of the mediums that I work in is group therapy so when we open new groups, when we interview our clients, members of the group and probably 60% of them, maybe 70% of the people we work with will have exactly that same fear or that sort of judgement of lack of worthiness, fear of being rejected, a fear of being really seen, sense of it doesn't feel safe.

It's about being okay to bring all of our sense of unworthiness and all of our sense of unsafety. Maybe for the first time it has a rightful place where it can be met, sat with, understood, and maybe even grieved. As we share our deep authentic feelings then trust starts to grow, and a sense of value starts to take root within the individual.

Group esteem starts to develop which can then influence the individual's sense of self-esteem and then slowly these things shift to where a lack of worth is gradually replaced with feeling they are a part of something, have a sense of belonging.

So, often people have all these fears, these sort of very normal avoidance strategies and unconscious sort of wants to pull back into the dull safety of an unfilled life.

These borrowed ideals and pains from our past that still haunt us in the present. When shared with another and in a group, where they can be really met, understood and at times challenged with heart.

Then maybe something new can happen or a door that was never there before can appear.

It is up to the individual if they want to step through that doorway into something new and that something new is not being alone. Bring it in. Gradually, something new can happen that definitely would not happen if you were alone.

Laura:

What do you feel is at the core of suffering?

Nigil:

When I first started working in the realms of addiction, society over the years has really looked down upon these people who are using drugs and alcohol in ways that were improper. Through a journey of really understanding, I feel it is actually not a disease (which is often what people call addiction) but through my experience it really was people having deep seated, unexpressed pain that is waiting to be held.

I really believe it's waiting to be held, to be not judged, to be leaned into with others, and not just spoken about, but spoken from.

This way the pain can educate the body, the brain, the heart and then help the individual grow in some developmental, behavioural, relational, physiological, and of course emotional way.

It's really about building the safety to allow the pain to come up, the suffering to come up and for it to move through this acknowledgement.

I feel that the root of suffering is unexpressed pain and the journey it takes to create the safety to allow another person to be there with us in those places we least want to go to. When we can do this then there can be a shaping, a reforming, and a changing of the suffering.

It goes through a journey, this is a journey that ripens and creates the possibility of flowering for the individual, where suffering can, through the alchemy of the body and the connection with the people who are allowed in, allowing for a change in the individual.

I really believe that suffering is the way, it's the doorway. It's where the unbearable can become bearable. Suffering is the cost of unexpressed pain that keeps showing up and haunting us. It echoes through our life until we're ready and capable to allow it to move into a new pattern that can be more nourishing than the old one.

Laura:

Do you believe there is a divine purpose to suffering?

Nigil:

From what I have witnessed, people grieving from places that they never knew existed, being held in the presence or in the arms of another person, then what What I witnessed is divine.

What I have witnessed is so beautiful that I could weep with my whole body to know that's what is possible in a human relationship, where we can have two hearts open to meet the struggle.

I think that spirit moves through people when they are open to this, and to me that definitely comes underneath the umbrella of a divine intervention or a divine happening.

I could never hold back the tears in moments that I have observed like this, because it is a spiritual or a divine experience - the beauty of connection.

Laura:

What is your definition of divinity in the way you were expressing it?

Nigil:

It's when there's an ordinary embodiment, where two people or a group of people are present to an unfolding, and there is a presence that comes forth from a cocktail of different things.

It's presence and it is an ability for an ordinary person to have their heart open a little bit, amongst the group or amongst the individual. It's the commitment of the people involved to want to keep being curious. There's a divine happening when you bring people together who are curious and want to grow.

When people are courageous and want to come out of the dull safety of an unfulfilled life and move into the unknown and uncertainty, something in that creates an atmosphere that is divine.

For me I feel divinity comes in in these experiences of togetherness and closeness, which then invokes a sense of connection. It's in the closeness, the togetherness, and the connection with people who choose to go into the unknown or navigate uncertainty within themselves in the unknown where a divine spirit can move through us and amongst us when we're courageous to do this.

Laura:

Do you feel it's possible for someone to feel the intimacy of what you've just described in and of themselves? Or do you feel this is necessary to experience with another?

Nigel:

In this time, and this age, I believe that we can experience a certain sort of connection to the spiritual landscape by yourself, a connection to something other, absolutely by yourself.

However I am more aware in these last years and especially through this pandemic where isolation, lack of movement, a severing of connection, and being all alone now more than ever, that we can remember and find new meaningful ways to be with one another. To learn to dwell with one another and learn how instead of living for other people, we can learn to be with other people in new ways that are heart centred, vulnerable, real and honest.

Yes you can have this connection by yourself with the divine. However, right now I think the world needs to come back and through this collective ordeal where we have been pulled away from one another, to help us to really remember our longings of what it means to be in a reliable and responsive community, because for a long time we've become very overly self-reliant.

We've become distant and isolated, as people. I think there is an invitation to come home to this thing called 'otherness', through connection. Not just with ourselves but with others. To create this possibility where we can lean in with other people and not be alone with our suffering,and not be alone with our pain.

For a long time collectively this has been a huge problem. When people isolate, when they avoid, and when they move away from other people, these are red flags that something is being avoided. There is some pain that has happened in the collective or in that individual's family structure.

One way to help us with our suffering is to reach and connect to this atmosphere with others. Sometimes one person might go where another person isn't able to go and can then take them with them.

They give them courage; they give them strength. When they see someone they resonate with going to that unknown territory of their emotional body, and when we bear another person's vulnerabilities, we bear our own, we don't need people just for relating, we need people for our very existence.

For us to deepen and for us to remember who we are.

I think what's really needed now is togetherness and closeness.

Laura:

Imagine a person who has only experienced isolation and aloneness, and who has not felt the receptivity or tenderness of a vulnerable share. What would be one thing that you could suggest that they could begin with as they reach out to others?

What could be an entry point, a baby step, a gesture, a prayer, or an intention that you can move someone closer to connection and togetherness?

Nigil:

People get to a place where they have to make a choice in their lives to hang out in the familiar, depressive, dark, habitual suffering and try to find comfort in that, or move into a place that feels equally scary and daunting in the direction of something new and unknown.

There will be people that are going to be able to make a new choice, and some will not choose to. In the beginning of my work, I had this fantasy that everybody would, but that is not the case.

A small step that anybody could start to take would be to begin journaling how they are with themselves, whether that's painting, whether that's writing, or whether that's dancing.

They can dance how they feel, or they paint how they feel or write down how they feel and this becomes witnessed by a higher part of them. It's witnessed by spirit, it's witnessed by their future selves that have not fully come into fruition yet. The prayer is the honoring of what is there.

The struggle of this, whatever that is for them, whether it's loneliness or body image issues, depression or trauma that's showing up in their relationships, or they've chosen to be out a relationship because it's just so painful to be in one, or it's an accident that happened, a disability or illness, as humans nobody escapes the vulnerabilities of what it means to be a human.

Whatever it is, I think just acknowledging what is happening, can be the first step that can create movement. That movement can be a thousand different steps that can come after the first step of saying yes this is what's here, it's not easy and it's painful.

Laura:

The Buddhist's have said that pain is inevitable, and suffering is optional. How do you feel about that statement?

Nigil:

I love that. I love that because I think suffering happens and continues to happen when we hang out in an isolated world of our own minds, when we continually collapse in our pain. That is suffering.

I think by allowing us to speak from the suffering and to share that and not be alone with it, can allow something different to happen than what we experienced in our childhood.

As an adult to have this new experience, to have somebody there with you, to help you to feel safe in the feeling. Then you can allow that pain or the suffering to be grieved through the pain and know that you're not collapsing. You can then move out of that loop.

Suffering can be a loop - the same thing, different faces, different places but the same heartache, again and again and again. By grieving the pain we end the suffering.

We grow an ordinary capacity to be with the intensity of feelings and emotions, and grow our ability to have more resilience as humans, not to avoid but to feel, to digest, and to awaken through our bodies, through our feelings, through our hearts, through our loves and our losses.

It's only when we can feel our pain that we can start to understand ourselves. When we can feel into our suffering, we begin to better understand ourselves in the context of our relationships. We can gradually make more informed, healthier and adapted choices based on a deeper awareness of our own feelings and patterns.

By grieving the suffering we move into the acceptance of what it is and in the presence of others it can help us to cultivate trust and authenticity. By taking responsibility through this whole process, we are able to strengthen our emotional intelligence.

The Buddhist's worked this out a long time ago. When we go into pain, we can stop our suffering.

Laura:

What do you feel is the antithesis of suffering? When the suffering ends, what would the desired outcome and life experience be?

Nigil:

From my experiences you would be able to better deal with all of life's ups and downs, heartaches and heartbreaks, hurts and pains, and be able to move through them.

It's not that you're going to extinguish the pain, but you would be better prepared to deal with life. You would be able to then probably lean into life more and engage with it instead of avoiding it.

If there's a suffering cycle happening we tend to avoid life and hang out in the very familiar dull safety of an unfulfilled life, held hostage by the suffering and haunted habitual happenings that keep us stuck or frozen into these ways of being.

When we break through that we lean into life, we engage, and engagement is the key here.

Engagement into life and taking a risk that something new could happen, a movement towards something new, towards the other, towards life. By grieving the suffering, we open up the possibility to say yes to life in new ways.

Laura:

Have you ever considered ending your own life?

Nigil:

In my life there were plenty of times where I was in the slow suicide of avoiding life and really deadening my life for sure. As a child I came from an environment where I was starved of connection, presence, guidance, emotional awareness that kept me hungry., was depleted from the things that are essential to the aliveness of life. This birthed a desire for me to want to grow.

There was a desire in me from a young age to know that something isn't right here, a desire, a sort of longing to know that it can't be like this. As a teenager, I was deeply troubled, and came from a troubled landscape called my family.

My parents were beautiful people and good people, and they did the best they could, but their lights both emotionally and relationally were switched off.

Both were blue collar workers and I was expected to do the same, however things didn't go the way my father wanted it. Through the early stages in my life, I had a lot of struggles with addiction. I had a lot of struggles with relationships and I felt as if I was dying.

I felt deeply anxious and nervous all the time, with periods of deep depression which felt like a slow suicide. There was one moment I remember where there were so many emotions that came up. I was by myself and was walking back to my little cottage, and the immensity of the pain was in every step and I could feel the excruciation of the loneliness, the emptiness, the heartbreak in my body of the life that I was living.

There was a moment where I entertained the idea of ending my life. I was coming around a corner on a very busy road. I walked out onto that road and into a blind corner, a 90-degree corner and I knew a car was coming but a voice within me said, "Nigil. Step onto the path now."

I did and in that moment a car just came around and the mirror of the car just stroked my arm as it flew around the corner at nearly 50mph. I was shaking on the side of the road and I wept. In that moment, I think like most suicides there are parts of us which we want to kill.

There's these parts of us that we want to kill off but what I discovered in the weeks and the months after that, that I could grieve these parts and move them through my system. Also sharing with other people , then these parts that I wanted to kill helped to build my ground, my sense of myself and then my heart opened.

I was really shaped in the process. Years later, I can sit with people who are suicidal and go back to that memory. Back to the time when I wanted to kill parts of myself and my suicidal attempt.

This then somehow allows the other to sit with and grieve those parts that's so hard to live with, whether it's shame, guilt, loneliness or just how life doesn't seem to be fair sometimes, but to grieve that.

Then the breakdown has the possibility of being a breakthrough, to something new, something different, something vastly bigger than what you could imagine when you're in it.

That was a pivotal moment in my life, things really started to heat up after then in a good way.

Laura:

What powerful symbology from your inner voice that said 'step onto the path'.

Why do you feel so many of the younger generations are committing suicide at this time?

Nigil:

Any time a child has any sort of mental health problem it's due, almost entirely due to a non-responsive environment around them. Suicide is an extreme reaction to a child or a teenagers inability to live with the despair, the struggle, the pain, or the suffering of some part of them that they want to kill off, which plays out in a suicide attempt or an actual suicide.

What creates this influx is a continuation and a continuum of family environments that are non-responsive and non-reliable. This is due to the mom and dad, or the circle of influence not being attuned to their pain and suffering.

Being unable to be attuned to their children, or perhaps also contributing to the struggles of their children due to their styles of relating as well as their inability to be with their company, be curious, and be interested in the interior world of their children.

I think in the world at large we need to start to create communities, small communities where they are responsive and reliable, where they can learn to talk about the struggles instead of burying them, where they can learn to lean into the pain instead of needing to medicate them. We can be with each other in ordinary ways that can help us bear the unbearable before the unbearable ends another child's life. That's my belief.

Laura:

What do you feel is a solution for parents who are dealing with her own sense of overwhelm to be more available for their children's needs?

Nigil:

A huge problem in the world today with parenting is that parents are mostly terrified of their children. They pander to them often. In ways where they're not able to be with them, they give them stuff. They leave them for long periods of time. They are unable to deal with their own sort of pain and suffering, so they work really hard to not allow their children to be in touch with theirs either. This has been going on for a long time. I would welcome all parents to read the work of Donald Winnicott, from the 70s, he used to have a BBC and is a psychoanalyst.

He used to have a BBC show, ahead of its time in the 70s, talking to parents, to help them cultivate the idea of being a good enough parent. Perfect parents generally want to give their kids' stuff and hide, overwhelm the parents, and deaden the child. So, it is about how to become a 'good enough parent'.

What goes for the children also goes for the adults where they find responsive, reliable environments to be able to talk about their pain and struggles, where they can get resources outside of their own thinking about what needs to happen.

So, whether that's group therapy, individual therapy, working on one or two friends getting together. There is an opportunity to really deepen here with one and other into the unknown of their feelings instead of just, "I'm okay." and learn to birth the sort of philosophy to- "no I'm not okay and that is okay".

They are able to allow themselves, in an ordinary way, to get to know themselves so they can learn to then get to know their children. Learn to evolve out of a style of living that they learned from their families, and often bestow upon their children.

We all get contamination from our parents, but we can learn to notice them, lean into them, be imperfect with it, get it wrong, try again and develop along the way. It's all about being supported, the secret is support.

Parents can be really supportive for their children when they're supported. There's lots of ways, emotionally, where parents can be supported.

Laura:

Do you feel social media has a role in the increase of suicide?

Nigil:

It used to be magazines, it used to be television, and we can't blame a whole system of marketing, but definitely it creates these illusions of people showing their best parts of themselves and not showing the struggle.

They see mannequins of how to live and they don't see or know the pain behind them and then are ill-equipped to deal with their own sort of struggles as they mature.

It is not helpful but there needs to be a parental figure, and chaperones for children that can reiterate - "Yes that's nice that you can have these material things and it's nice to have the make-up and to have the dresses.

There's nothing wrong with that. But there's so much more to you than what you look like. Let's talk about how you feel." As long as it's supportive orientations and parents not forgetting about their children because there's a lot of difference than feeding and giving money to your children that rearing a child.

To raise a child, to really take a deep interest in them, not just play with them, but witness them. So, as a whole invitation that, hey these things are going to keep happening in the world of social media.

But have we got chaperones as parents who take a deep interest in our children to help them work through these sort of entrapments, these illusions of things that are not real and to help them come back to, "Okay well I can have the fast car but can I talk about my insecurities that the fast car might want to be superficially hide" for example, or "If I get 50 likes versus 1,000 likes."

What's been fuelled here? Where there's a curiosity about these things that validate us and how they also at the same time whilst fuelling the need for that. So, this curiosity of the internal world, of the children, is super important for adults to make the time for the kids and I suppose that only happens if they make time for themselves.

Laura:

Why do you feel that men commit suicide more so than women?

Nigel:

I believe from my work with men it is because an archetypal fathers vulnerability was not on top of the list. Authenticity was not on top of the list. Being sensitive was not on top of the list. We have contaminated beliefs like boys don't cry, don't show your weakness.

As for women, they should be seen and not heard, all these old contaminations of ways of living which don't work. They don't work in many ways but one of the ways is that life just becomes too much when we're having to hold it all in, or internal realities that corrupt our minds that really beat us up inside. Then, after a while it feels like life is not worth living because we've been told to neglect parts of ourselves that start to shout and become louder, so confused.

So often fathers, fathers, fathers, pass on belief systems regarding not needing to worry about feelings, you just have to keep pushing forward. The reality is that this doesn't work, we all need to challenge these outdated ideals.

Whether it's a slow suicide like a work addiction or a quick suicide like the things that are happening in the world today. Men need to be vulnerable.

Laura:

What do you feel is an intersection and healthy balance between vulnerability and strength?

Nigil:

I think deep vulnerability is strength. Deep vulnerability is a deep strength, We all have different degrees of atrophy, and certain muscles, to develop that strength in our vulnerabilities, the bare nakedness. We all as a species we have to keep working on.. We all have become way too accustomed to being really independent. Such a terrible affliction that protects the vulnerability which is to me the strength.

I'm not saying everybody needs to be crying on street corners either, which is collapsing. Strength is being present in the face of our vulnerabilities and our pain, and we keep saying yes to life anyway. We keep moving forward, and engaging. What does it take to engage with life more? That's strength.

Both strength and vulnerability are required to live a full life, not one or the other. That's one quality of strength, saying yes to life. Another form of strength is doing the right thing sometimes, naming something when it's much easier to not name it.

Again, it comes back to being open, and undefended and vulnerable and putting yourself at risk, you know that people might reject you. Maybe 10 people have to have passed the dog on the road, and maybe you just could do it as well because you're rushing and you could actually have the strength to say, "You know what, I'm going to stop and pick up this dog, and change the course of my day. Change the course of the dog's life as well."

That takes a lot of strength and courage to do something like. That's maybe not the best analogy but there's so many things that accumulate the strength but the one that stands out for me is the strength to bear it all and to still move forward in life, and to look at the things that hinder that progress to more fuller engagement.

Laura:

Your analogy reminds me interestingly enough of a social media video that garnered almost 50million views. The video was a woman who stopped her car on a very busy highway and you can't tell what she is stopping for. She waves her hands to stop the cars coming on the busy highway. The next thing you see is a pheasant or a bird of some sort walking across the road with 12 of its baby chicks. I feel like the reason that video got so much traction is because of this deeper part of ourselves that recognises that ability to prioritize life in this way.

Nigil:

Yes, if we can slow down enough to appreciate the need to be in connection and regard for every living being, not just lost in our own swamp of our own minds, unable to notice and smell and touch. The beauty of seeing those chicks walking across the road, there is humanity in that. If we are not slowed down enough and we're not resourced enough, it's hard to imagine how they could be important.

Laura:

What is your definition of vulnerability?

Nigil:

For me vulnerability is allowing the world to see parts of you that you have learned not to love.

Through allowing another person to see what you have learned not to love, you can start to re-shape what you think about what you once learned not to love, through how they react to you. The person who's observing you, is also learning to bear their own vulnerabilities while bearing yours, so this wonderful thing starts to mushroom through the experience.

This potential of an atmosphere of change that happens when when we are owning up to your own inner truths versus being lost in your own illusions and fantasies is a vulnerability of sorts, however the one I'm talking about is where there is you and another person, or you and a group, and it creates an atmosphere of the possibility of something new to happen.

Laura:

Having traveled the world extensively and connecting with many indigenous cultures and shamans, is there one in particular that comes to mind and heart, that spoke to a solution for suffering?

Nigil:

This comes from my early years of being a student of an Uzbekistan Sufi, and it still rings true today. The words she used to say to me, "You've got to stop trying to look for this great love in your life. You need to start looking for all the ways that you block letting that love in. Until you do that, you're going to continually suffer and you're not going to evolve."

That transmission from her is still in every single sort of daily meditation. where I look at humbly, honestly and authentically all of the ways that I stop letting love in. This helps to birth acceptance, self-acceptance, self-responsibility, and really strengthens the part where we can be imperfect humans living an evolving conscious journey.

Where we can notice the ways we go off on familiar patterns around how we avoid, slowly just coming home again and re-shaping as we go.

It's not about finding this great love, it's about how we stop letting love in, that creates a lot of suffering and illusion. For me it is to come out of the fantasy and start to look with open eyes, not just in the head but the heart of the reality of our own existence.

Laura:

A Journey Back to Self.

> *Nigel McFarland is a Group & Psycho-energetic Therapist with more than 17 years experience and is one of the founders of Wellbeings.*

For More Info:

Wellbeings.ie

WINGING IT WITH RICKI LAKE

Ricki:

After Christian committed suicide, I was a mess for a while. The thing that healed me or began me on my healing path was a reading I did with a psychic. I had that reading almost on the year anniversary of Christian's death. Christian died on February 11th, 2017, I first read with her in January, the end of January 2018.

And I did it begrudgingly. Because I have access to physics and to mediums I did it all on my show and when Christian died, I had this physic I reached out to and she told me where his body was and we were able to find Christian because of the information he gave to her.

I believe very strongly that our loved ones are still here and that there are ways to tap in and connect to them, whether through our meditation, or dreams and also through gifted mediums.

I had a friend recommend an incredible psychic, when I was at my lowest.

I went into the phone session basically rolling my eyes on a blocked number, the psychic didn't know anything about who I was or who I wanted to connect with. She needed my middle name and my age, that was all she needed and when I tell you, I mean that reading, it was Christian, he spoke to me for an hour.

He corrected her at times, she's like, "Do you want to talk to Pamela?" He's like, "Yes I do but that's not her name. Her name is --" And he kept saying, she's like. "It's a sound-a-like, it's a sound-a-like its Ricki." Cause I'm asking him can you spell it? And he spells out, "R-I-C I see the C K-I. It's Ricki or something, Ricki. Am I butchering your name?"

I said, "Oh my God that's him. That's me. That's me." The details she provided had me a total believer in the ability to connect with the other side.

The detail, the detail of who he was in a past life, he was a native American from North Western New Mexico and he worked with Navajo.

He worked with Native American jewellery; he was a trader. He was a fourth-generation trader from New Mexico, so he was in his last lifetime before , when his brother's name was Shela, and he saved his brother's life.

There was a bear, the native American Navajo word is "shash", and he describes the whole thing as this bear/shash was up on its hind legs about to attack his brother and he distracted the bear. His brother then ran off and was saved, but Christian was killed by the bear. His brother mourned the loss of him so deeply he promised that he would be with him when he came into this next lifetime. So Christian told the psychic, "When I came into this earth life on July 24th, 1971 (which is his birthday), in North Western, New Mexico, it was my brother Shela who guided me."

He spoke about taking his life, where he was, what he was feeling. He said many things and one of the first things he said was, "I want you to know you are my wife and I will never say that I'm not married to you." Because we were divorced, I had to divorce him. He said, "You're my wife and I will never say that I'm not married to you." So many details.

The psychic knew nothing about me. It was so specific. She spoke about his dog Pascha. She couldn't get the name, she's like, "Patcha, Patcha, Pascha. It's an Indian name. It's a bulldog." It was so specific and literal.

My mind was blown.

Laura:

One of the things that's going to perhaps come up in the mind of the reader, in the time of Google, is that somebody could research all this so what would you say to any of the sceptics?

Ricki:

She did not know who I was. I called on a blocked number. She didn't know my name. She didn't know anything about me. I made sure when I was booking it, I was like I don't want her to know anything and then I talked, and she was 81. You know? I talked to her nine months later on my birthday, which was our anniversary as well. We got together on my birthday.

The first reading blew my mind and completely set me on this path of healing and the knowing that he is always with me.

I know he is always with me. Even with my new partner being here, Christian is overseeing, he is orchestrating, he is watching over me because I took care of him. I know it was a promise he made to me that he was going to look after me, and I know I'm protected by him.

So, I just listened to the other two readings just like two weeks ago here in my new house. I just moved into this house. This is the house I found with Christian, I was building it for both of us, his ashes are here. He is here.

In this space that I'm in now, this is my bedroom, I have pictures of him with his arms outstretched, the way he always posed, with his arms out. I would take a picture from the back, and there is a picture of him and me holding him, in the centre of this room.

I know what I know. I know what I'm experiencing with my connection. I know how powerful Christian Evan is over on the other side.

Christian's body, his brain, his everything didn't work on this plane but where he is now, I believe he is helping everyone. He is doing the work that he always wanted to do here. He always wanted to help people and be of service. I just know it.

I was really struggling for a really long time, self-medicating and throwing myself into things. I was flailing and just feeling so lost. How could this happen to me? How could I have lost my favorite person in the world? I'm a saviour. I'm a manifester. I am someone that can handle my shit and I couldn't save him.

I struggled for so long and this woman through that first reading just gave me this knowing, this knowing that he is always here. There's just been one thing after another and just lately being in this home he's shown himself again.

One of the signs is 11 11. He took his life on the 11th of the 11th month. He sent the note at 1:11. It's just always been like I see 11 11 all the time and I know a lot of people do but just a couple of weeks ago I played through those two other recordings.

The second one where he talked, he's with Carol and Norma, his grandparents. Everything was so specific. It was for sure him.

It's mind blowing to anyone who knows the details. Cut to the third reading, I was listening to them here by myself. It was the first time I was at home by myself. I spent the day just listening, out by my pool, looking at the ocean, listening to these readings.

I was relaying it to my best friend the next day who came to see the house for the first time, it was just the two of us, and I'm telling her what was said in this reading and she immediately gets a phone call. She picked up her phone, and she has something called a Ring, which is an alarm system where if someone is at your front door and you're not at home, you get a phone call and you can see who's at the front door.

She picks up her phone it's 1:11. No one was at the door. No one was there. Just then the TV that was on pause went to black, and turned off.

Then, she jumps up, and freaks out. She said "oh my god. Oh my God." and I said it's Christian. It's Christian showing himself right now." She had goose bumps everywhere!!. I said, "That's Christian. That's Christian."

She was on one side of my huge living room and she looked across at a pile of books because my bookcase isn't built yet. She said one book is sticking out to me, I don't even know what that is.

She walks over, and picks up the book, which is called Spirit Hacking by Shaman Durek. She doesn't know Shaman Durek and didn't know that he did that ceremony for Christian. We just absolutely knew Christian was with us. This type of thing happens a lot!

Also, when Christian died, we couldn't find his body, and so I called another medium and told her that we couldn't find his body and that I needed her help. She said, "It's Christian, isn't it?" I said, "Yes." So, she told me where he was, we found his body and she said, "He wants you to have the ring. He wants to have the ring."

On Valentine's Day in 2017, three days after he died, I went on this wild goose chase to find his wedding band. The wedding band that he had pawned.

I found it in a pawn shop and it was so dramatic, I collapsed when I found the ring. He wanted me to have the ring.

Four years later,it was my first night in this new home that I had built with Christian or had seemingly built with Christian on my side. I was with my man, Ross, and we were in our jacuzzi for the first night that we were here and he asked to marry him very spontaneously, Which referenced what Christian had said which was that he wants me to have the ring. It was so clear to me that Christian was with us.

It has all been such a gift, the blessings that have come out of the relationship with Christian, the love, the loss and now knowing that he is still with me. He is still with me and us.

Laura:

What would you say to someone who has lost their loved one to suicide that's very much in the grief state and guilt state?

Ricki:

I don't know what I would say. I would just share my story, I never had a guilt state. I did not feel guilty. I never asked why, I knew why. I had lived with his struggle and his suffering day in and day out.

I knew that it was very hard for him to be in his skin and in his mind. Yes, it was shocking, but I wasn't surprised, as I knew there was a chance of that. When I met him, he was suicidal. I saved Christian's life twice. When

I first got together with him and then years later after the first episode, I saved him, I couldn't save him the third time.

I needed to save myself, I needed to cut myself loose from this cycle. I do feel like sharing my story to people that will listen, continues me on my path of healing and I think it gives, it offers hope, yes.

Laura:

What do you feel is the soul contract that you and Christian have?

Ricki:

Christian would say it all the time that we were together for something greater than just us.

I believe in eternal love, love is eternal and that even if they're not here in physical form they're just as present. Christian is here and of course I wish he was here in physical form, but I also look at what I have now and what I have now is so much healthier.

I think the big piece for me with Christian with loving him and losing him, was for me to have learned to love myself the way Christian loved me.

I now value myself and so that's why I was able to manifest someone that is worthy of me, my time, my love, my gifts, you know?

Yes, Christian was a total gift to me, I am so grateful.

I never thought I'd be where I am now, this has really been the turn of events that I didn't expect. They say time heals and all of that and I suffered for a long, a long time but I also managed to keep my heart open through it. The pain was as deep as the love.

Laura:

What was causing your suffering?

Ricki:

Just the loss. That this wasn't how my story was supposed to end. I get everything you want. I'm a manifester, and I've always managed to really land on my feet. I jump and I land on my feet for the most part, so when Christian and I met and fell in love, I mean I thought it was my happily ever after, I really did. But life was a struggle for him. I couldn't make him happy, I couldn't take his pain away.

I couldn't make him believe in himself by saying that I loved him. He would say to me, "If only I could love myself the way you love me or see myself the way you see me." I just couldn't give that to him, and I forgive him. I understand, I understand, and I think that's part of why he's been able to soar and do as well as he is doing over there, wherever he is, apparently, he's in the third heaven.

He said he's in third heaven and that he has a chance to move up but he's happy, he's at peace, he feels like himself, he said the only thing is he doesn't have me,

Laura:

I think there's something really significant that you just shared about realising you couldn't save him, and you couldn't make him happy because I think there's a lot of people that feel that there's something that they can do to keep somebody on the planet.

Is there anything else that you could offer in terms of wisdom that could just help liberate somebody who's feeling the aftermath of having a loved one end their life? There are a lot of people that feel that they are somehow responsible, and the guilt piece comes in. I wish I could have done something, or if only I had _____.

Ricki:

It's a very helpless feeling because we are all responsible for our own happiness.

I'm dealing with my younger son who is 19 and he's struggling with mental health issues.

He's had a lot of loss including his stepfather, Christian, and he's struggling.

He's struggling right now, and I think it's chemical, you know, he's trying to figure out his meds and all of that. He's in a dire situation. It triggers me because of course with Christian I had access to doctors, access to everything, I put him in a treatment centre, he was on a 5150 hold.

I mean there's only so much you can do and so I go to that place with my child wanting to fix it and there's only so much I can do. I'm here for him, always here and we will figure it out and this too shall pass, but it is really hard when your loved one is struggling like that and you want to fix it. Ultimately that person needs to find their way to their own happiness.

In the case of Christian, I don't think Christian was meant for this world, he just was otherworldly. He would always say he's an alien and I know he stayed as long as he did for me. I do believe he spared me because I think it would have gotten worse and he knew it was going to get worse.

I'm now with someone who is as happy as I am, who wakes up happy and isn't in pain,and is a whole person. We are very compatible. I have found true love again

Laura:

This can be such a beacon of hope for people that are in the aftermath of losing a intimate partner to suicide, to be able to see the shining example of this true love reflection that can be cultivated in life with an open heart and forgiveness. You still can still be happy ever after.

You played a vital role in this, allowing yourself to feel love again after the "loss".

What would you say are the main ingredients that really helped you to move on and move into a state of continuing to allow love in your life, as well as maintaining connection to Christian?

Many people can shut down when something like this happens, however you can choose to stay as an instrument of love and hope.

Laura:

Knowing what you know about Christian's continued spirit and presence in your life, what is your current relationship to suicide?

Ricki:

I mean, it just feels so prevalent right now. It just, you know, it was something that I mean I thought about it because obviously when I was with Christian, I met him, he was suicidal when we met, and he had told me and shared with me that he was making a choice not to because he fell in love with me and made a commitment to me.

So, I mean it just seems to be everywhere, it seems like it's just, you know, and obviously with the state of the world, it's just so hard to be human, so I understand it. I never was suicidal, but I definitely had moments of like I don't want to be here, I never would, like I never had a plan, but it was just so painful just to get up and get out of bed in the morning.

I didn't understand depression until I lost Christian. I lived with it. I lived with him being depressed and physically in pain and not able to wake up and be motivated. It was after he died, there were months where I just didn't want to. I just was completely unmotivated and shut down and isolated and I felt so alone. It was so lonely. The stigma and the shame. I started to feel sorry for myself. After a few months after Christian's death, everyone's life continued and I just felt stuck. I had my dog who forced me to get out and get out in the sun.

I just forced myself one foot in front of the other, to go to the beach. I lived at the beach, I went to the beach every day, I'd smile at the sun. I'd force myself to just be grateful, look at the blessings I have in my life. It was literally like one foot in front of the other and it was a very lonely experience, even though I did have a support system.

Laura:

I think this is so important to remove the stigma of suicide and depression and to continue to fortify that you not alone in this. Public figures and famous people also face depression and despair and feel alone and see that even with friends, even with money in the bank, and even with a "healthy body".

Everyone faces their own inner demons , which ultimately can be the catalyst for their own journey back to Self.

Ricki:

I also want to add that many people think that it's a selfish act and I actually feel in my case it's the opposite, I think it was a very selfless act for him to make that choice and I think it's a very brave choice. It is not easy to take your life. People can feel so angry when someone they know ends their life.

Milo, my older son, was so angry with Christian, but I never felt that. But one thing I do want to add is that I suffered from Sciatica. I never had it before, and I got it literally overnight. I could not walk, my whole right side, I don't know if you've ever had it but it basically it's so painful. I didn't know where it was coming from.

I was on a hit show called The Masked Singer.. You had to be completely anonymous and no one knew it was me, so I had to wear weighted costumes every time I did it. I was in dire pain and I was about to go to Burning Man for the first time, not the second time.

I was desperate as I couldn't walk. I ended up reading a book by Doctor Sarno, Healing Back Pain. In it he discusses how our nervous system, and our brain and our bodies are connected.

What I figured out was it was repressed rage towards Christian for taking his life and leaving me. I never felt rage, I never thought I was angry with him, but my body was internalising this.

So, I began what's called a journal speak and I basically would write 20-minutes a day where you just throw up, like you're a five-year-old having a temper tantrum of just like fuck it, I fucking hate whatever, whatever you say, it is a release and it just gets it out of your body. It was a really powerful exercise and I healed myself from my Sciatica.

I have never had it again, and it was just really interesting to come to terms with the fact that even though I didn't feel angry towards him outwardly, I was carrying it internally.

Laura:

Yes, absolutely! Moving it out of the body on a cellular level is so important.

To recap what you shared earlier - not feeling that suicide is selfish, but it's actually a selfless act and it requires a lot of courage for someone to make that choice.

Ricki:

Yes, and follow through. It was helpful to know through the medium that I had sessions with, where Christian's head was at.

He was so lost, and she said, "Was he drinking?" And Christian didn't drink alcohol but I'm sure he was on pills. He had voices in his head that were telling him, and he couldn't stop the voices, that he went in this tunnel once he did, he had shot himself in the head. She knew that. She was asking him how he killed himself, but she didn't want to upset him.

He said a light went off in his head and that the minute he did it, he tried to go back, but couldn't. He kept going down a tunnel. The way he was describing it sounded like a slide. I envisioned it like a tunnel, a dark tunnel and he was trying to climb back, he was trying to climb back but he couldn't.

Then there was a light and then there was a figure that showed itself and he said, "Is this you?" He said it wasn't my face, it wasn't Ricki, it was his brother from another lifetime. He didn't have a brother here, and his brother was named Sheila. "Shela." She kept saying "Shela" And then she said "Shash." And shash is bear in Navajo. He was a Navajo Indian and had saved his brother's life, and this bear the shash, and it was this bear claw, and I was like it's another message of wanting me to have this ring.

Laura:

Is there anything else that you feel called to share before we complete?

Ricki:

I haven't figured it all out yet but what has unfolded for me through this, through this journey with Christian has been my greatest teacher.

Laura:

What has it taught you?

Ricki:

That love is eternal, and that self-love is where it all starts. That life is precious and beautiful. and yes, I am such an example of someone who has come from the darkest of days, back into the light, and am now in a place of such abundance and self-love.

I am getting everything I deserve. I have worked really hard on myself; I've worked really hard. I am a good person; I have gone through a lot and there are so many gifts that come out of the trauma and the darkness.

It is the agony, the ecstasy, it all goes hand in hand. It goes back to my birth work, and the movies I make. Birth is a perfect analogy, it's like you can't have the ecstasy without some of the agony and that's true in life and love. I'm so grateful to have had Christian.

I am sad that it didn't last longer and that I didn't have him longer here, but I am a better human having gone through all of it.

Ricki Lake is an American actress, television presenter, producer and documentary filmmaker.

https://www.instagram.com/rickilake/

WINGING IT WITH
YASMEEN CLARK AND RAMAN PASCHA

Laura:

What do you feel is the cause of depression?

Yasmeen:

The one cause that Raman has taught me to understand and that he's really wanting to bring to the world is that we are essentially feeling beings, we feel our lives and in understanding our comprehension of our experience in life we come to understand it mentally.

So, it's essential for us to be able to know what it is we're feeling, to be able to process that really well and clearly. If that's too painful, if it's too traumatic, if it's something that cycles again and again very often people try not to feel and they begin to focus mentally primarily. That's really easy to do in our world because we're very physically, very mentally based and it can be very easy just to do things and just too logical and reasonable.

But there's a cost in there because we start overriding how we feel, and we inevitably begin to disconnect from ourselves. There is a disconnection between our thoughts and our feelings which ultimately need to work together, and that result is that we become stuck and that we don't have access to what we know or our inner voice.

It's difficult to reconcile ourselves with our experience and what we experience on the inside, and feeling, and what we're thinking about. So, ultimately disconnection. It has been shown a lot, I believe, in the world where connection is a deep cause in terms, or the lack of connection is a deep cause of addiction. It's equally implicated within our own relationship with ourselves.

Laura:

So the lack of connection to ourselves is the cause of addiction?

Yasmeen:

In our world at Pascha Therapies, our approach is that a lack of connection with our own inner voice, our own knowing, our own feelings, and that is the cause of depression.

Some have been really proving that the lack of connection to community, family, emotional support, participation in the world leads to addiction. That's really clear and Raman has been teaching and my role as a Pascha therapist also allows me to see how that lack of connection to yourself because of pain, because of trauma, because of feelings that we don't want to feel, they can seem so overwhelming means that we end up in our head and we get stuck there. The thoughts go around, and around, and around. They repeat and often people in severe depressive states or even in states of just wanting to stop their lives, they just want to stop feeling stuck.

They want to change what was happening and they just want to switch it off and escape it. Of course, the more we get stuck in our head, the worse often we feel, and it is attending to that feeling and having a good balanced flow between what we feel and think that brings about healing and wholeness again. We are not only thinking beings, we are beings who live life, and we feel, we sense, and we're sensitive and empathetic, and some people find that really hard.

Particularly if they've had pain and disappointment that hasn't healed or has really let them down in life.

Laura:

Is there a divine purpose to trauma?

Yasmeen:

That's an interesting question, Laura, a divine purpose? Trauma is the result of deep shock,or a prolonged event that renders someone incredibly vulnerable and forever changed and if there is not enough support for individuals in that state then of course it becomes deeply damaging and there is PTSD (Post Traumatic Stress Disorder).

The whole nervous system becomes shattered or becomes rendered and unable to function in a normal way. To say that this is a divine purpose I'm not sure in the immediate context, but what Raman is just telling me now is that in the healing process around trauma, there is an opportunity to recognise what is needed, and sometimes it's something that has been missing in someone's life that creates a bridge for them to heal, grow and to move forward, stronger from the experience to build on that experience.

So, we could say that is a divine purpose because it allows growth, it allows healing. In trauma it is necessary to acknowledge so deeply what has happened without blame and to really understand the deep vulnerability that people feel or fall into, and if that's not healed then they don't grow from it stronger, they just try to create ways of managing and coping.

Raman's saying that there's a deep, spiritual, divine purpose in the healing that is possible for us. Not that we necessarily are born to suffer trauma and therefore grow strong from it, but that this is a part of who we are as spiritual beings to learn to do it, to support each other, to do that in life. Not as a way of surviving life but as a way of understanding the world in which we're living and how to live in it well and survive some of the things that can happen in this world.

Laura:

What would you say is a core solution for depression?

Yasmeen:

One of the core solutions is to understand that as depression grows, (providing there is not too much medication to buffer and stop feeling) the healing of this is to recognise how slowly and gradually life gets small,

all the external things in life drop away, people find it hard to move, to be motivated, to get out of bed, to care for themselves.

The one core feeling that is often the most traumatic or uncomfortable is the one that actually needs to be connected with and heard. The solution resides in absolutely acknowledging everything that is being felt without judgement or criticism and learning to see what has really been needed.

Sometimes for depression, people will have managed, coped, survived so many things until there's just one thing too many and they give in, or they give up or it just feels too hard, and it really does depend on their awareness and how they see themselves or life.

So, it needs a lot of love and care, it needs someone able to see and recognise what is actually happening energetically for that person, what is happening spiritually, physically, mentally, emotionally for that person so that they can be held and supported to understand that this can heal, that it will change.

Unfortunately for many people, depression is something lived with for so long that it almost becomes fatalistic, progressively discouraging, disconnecting, and they just need to be led back with a huge amount of love and care. Those who are depressed give up on those things because their life isn't nourishing, supporting them. There's nothing to look forward to, life gets gradually smaller and darker.

They can of course put on a really bright face to the world, but their own life experience becomes smaller and smaller. So, until that one part of them feels seen, heard, accepted and there's consistent loving care and support around them they won't feel any sense of hope or oneness toward recovery.

In our culture prescriptions are given for antidepressants so easily, so quickly, often within the first 10 minutes of someone consulting with their doctor and barely is there any mention of counselling, or therapy, or form of support.

We tend to just medicate and help people function or medicate and try and block out the feelings that are difficult. We need to feel this, we need to listen to this and feel that we can, with the right support so that we don't fall into fear, or we don't fall into overwhelm. With love and consistency we can grow, we can heal through it.

Laura:

What could you say to someone that has cultivated enough awareness to realise there's something more than the depressing experience they've had? Someone who has been clouded or numbed down through the pharmaceutical medication they have been on? What could you offer in terms of just a next step, that could help them begin to free them from a co-dependency to that pharmaceutical and to that drug state?

Yasmeen:

There are two things that we offer, one is that we actually encourage people to look at either herbal or naturopathic options that don't have the disconnecting numbing down, fog–like feeling that people describe. Unless there has been a very big trauma and people need a little short-term buffer medically for that.

Of course, I haven't ever taken an antidepressant, so I personally don't know what it's like. But I've worked with a lot of people who have, and they talk about that numbness. So, actually moving toward naturopathic support, whatever form that takes, can give people a sense of feeling supported in their nervous system while a quiet, gentle, thawing out and waking up begins to happen within them.

The other thing that they can do is to listen to themselves and to do things each day that nourish and support them. Sometimes that can be so basic as being able and willing to get out of bed, to go sit out in the sunlight, listen to the birds, to shower, to eat something nourishing, to listen to music, to go for a walk. Not necessarily all at once but to begin looking after ourselves at a really basic level because our body suffers as well.

If people fall into depression their diet falls away, they're not moving so their physiological functions aren't very good and diet as we're learning in neuroscience, has a huge impact on our brain and on how we feel. What we are eating will influence our ability to have energy and to lift our mood, to be able to make physical shifts along with talking, listening to self, being guided, and supported to look at in that way also.

Laura:

What would you say to someone that is considering ending their life?

Yasmeen:

I would say to them that they can change how they're feeling without ending their life. That if they chose to end their life, they may feel a little relieved from the life experience that becomes relentless and difficult, but they don't necessarily change what it was they were feeling and struggling with inside.

What Raman talks about of course is that there is no sin, there is no spiritual punishment, there is tremendous support and healing for souls who suicide and we're seeing it more and more in the world, it's growing so hugely.

So, it's saying something huge about our cultures, our lifestyles, our lack of connection and support, people feeling isolated, turning inward, and never really feeling that they can say hey I'm struggling.

But when a person dies their soul will still know what they were feeling, and they will be encouraged to look at it to begin that healing process in spirit. So, it's not really an escape. It's not really a relief, well, sometimes it can feel the physical sensations of it are gone but there's part of us because it's our consciousness that we'll still need to look at and resolve whatever it was we fell into, whatever it was we got stuck in.

So, I would say somebody that in some ways is better for you to do it here, living but again you have to be prepared to help someone understand that the support is here and that what is required of them is do-able, that it's not too much, it's not asking too much, because by the time someone expresses that desire to end it, they've lost so much energy.

Laura:

Can you speak a bit more about what happens beyond the veil when someone ends their life?

Yasmeen:

What happens is that loved ones will be there as you might expect when anyone dies, spiritual guides, and loved ones draw close, that soul is really given all the love and care that they needed in life, that they had free will to choose to engage with or not.

That soul is welcomed, embraced and they're taken to a very beautiful environment that is really just full of energy. When we think of it, I guess if energy was coloured the environment would be vibrantly coloured in the most beautiful way, and they're held. So, their entire consciousness is held, and they are supported to recover depending on the method of death and they're also given constant, if we think of it in our human sense, it's round the clock, constant attention, someone with them, someone supporting them.

Often those who die, Raman talks about the realisation of what they've done, they become very conscious of those that are grieving and hurting because of what has happened, they become very concerned about that and about their loved ones. They're supported to recognise that process and what they may do in helping or supporting this.

But they're given absolute mega-doses of love in vibrational form because we're energetic beings and so if we were completed unfolded in the most beautiful energy we would relax, we would feel who we are and we would learn to see what was in life or what we chose or didn't do that allowed such a state of consciousness to occur, how we didn't feel empowered to process or reach out.

There's a lot for us to learn in that process but there's no sin, there's no religious sense of wrongdoing in that regard.

Yasmeen:

In life when you get depressed and when we're unhappy we become tense, we really tighten up and we shut down so we're not open, we're not receptive, and we gradually become a tight ball inside.

I think that's often what is depicted in art, in people curling up into a ball, turning in on themselves but not in a way that they're connecting but in a way that they're just holding.

So, in spirit, we get to unravel that, we get to really open up and we have that opportunity to learn and heal so that perhaps at another time life that aspect will be experienced in a different more empowered way.

But we're guided to do this individually because it is a very individual experience. It's not something that's just one size for all.

Laura:

For those that are left in the wake of a loved one that has committed suicide, what could you say to them to support their recovery process?

Yasmeen:

For the most part I would really clearly say to them that their grief will be feeling in some ways more painful because of the shock or surprise or the fact that they felt they'd tried to help, they may feel they failed.

I would simply say to them that even now their love matters because people often feel powerless and it is love that connects us between this world and the next, that never ends. So, I would say to them that it is actually their love that will reach the one who's gone, and that of course they will need to honour their grieving process.

But when someone takes their life, particularly, if it's a parent that has lost a child or a loved one whose partner has suddenly made a decision, there's a lot of grief but there's a lot of confusion and a lot of incomplete emotional processes between them and that other person.

So, you know, getting the support they need to be able to talk about it, to really trust their own process of healing and this is vital so they would need to do what the person who died was needing to do as well and that's to really ensure that there's a good connection between mentally processing what has happened physically but really deeply processing what they're feeling about that, with no inhibition, with no should and finding the support that they need for that.

I would also say to them that their love will be felt by their loved one and to talk to them, to share with them how they feel and for those who have lost loved ones particularly to suicide, there's often a lot of anger in that grief. There's a lot of upset that someone would do this. They struggle to understand how their loved one could just leave in that manner. It's not an easy situation at all.

Laura:

For those that have processed their grief and felt and met that on the other side of that those that are still here, anything that you could share with them that could support them to be in connection with their loved one that has crossed over?

Yasmeen:

After many years of working with spirit, I would encourage the awkwardness of those moments of suddenly thinking about their loved one and to know that it occurs, because they're standing right there with them at that moment.

Our entire energy system recognizes the energy of that soul who has passed, and to just give permission in that moment to register and acknowledge that they are there and to simply welcome them, to simply say. "Hi, I've missed you. I'm missing you. I'm grieving. I'm struggling". Whatever else it is, or even just in that moment to say, "Hi. I feel you. I feel you."

Often people talk about those random moments where their loved one comes into their mind and it's not random, it's merely a form of spiritual communication and as people learn to recognise that, they then learn that their loved one is seeking connection with them and they're seeking to assure them that they are still okay. I think that's one of the worst things for people when they lose their loved ones is that they don't know what's happened, and we have a lot of religious ideals around suicide, particularly in some church situations and that can be also equally devastating.

There's a desire for those on the other side to say, "I still exist. I still love you. I'm here." In those moments when people feel that loving presence, that's the connection, that's affirmation of eternal love, connection, still in existence.

Laura:

What would you say is the purpose of the mind?

Yasmeen:

The purpose of the mind is to absolutely comprehend and make sense out of what we feel and experience, we are sensory beings, and we don't have to think to know. Often, we just know and as we feel it, we begin to understand and comprehend and our mind is using reference points throughout our life, some reference points come from beyond this life and are more spiritual, but our mind is using reference points from past experience, even things we've known, experienced, felt, when we were younger.

Depending on whether that is positive, uncomfortable, negative, those reference points help us form a picture, a perception of what's happening, of what's going on, what we're experiencing. So, our mind is incredibly powerful and it's a wonderful vessel if you like for attaining awareness and knowledge, and our mind has a huge capacity to expand and to comprehend our reality in many different ways.

But it gets very narrow and is purely mentally driven, if we are only focused on the physical and on the thought and on conversation alone because we are spiritual beings first and foremost, our spiritual nature is equally present and our mind can struggle with that because conceptually it's difficult to have reference points, particularly if the mind is looking for proof physically as to that existence or not.

So, we have to experience many, what you might call, subtle energetic things that happen that are purely in the feeling realm before our mind says well actually this is not in the realm of everyday, this is in the realm of the soul. So, we have a spiritual language which is our feelings and then our mind absolutely learns through reference to compile awareness of our spiritual nature.

So, our mind is amazing, and we need both, we need to feel and think but the mind always does better when it's serving us, not when it's leading or being the master. If we're not connected to ourselves, our mind struggles and suffers and it imagines all sorts of things, it doesn't have the answers it needs and often the mind is asking and enquiring, questioning, and if we can't connect with and listen to ourselves the mind will ask other people, "I wonder what they think." That's not always successful either.

So, the mind is a part of us that we use when we're here in this world, when we're alive, and we need it but it's not ever going to be fully happy without our entire being.

Laura:

What would you say to someone who has relied on their mind and mental construct for their identity?

Yasmeen:

I would actually invite them to just take a breath and notice their experience in that moment, the part of them that is awake, aware, watching, conscious, witnessing and helping them to connect with that reality, which is purely in this moment, purely in this now, to get to know who that is.

I would encourage them to recognise what it is they know without thinking. I would ask them questions that they will realise immediately without thought and reconnect them with who they are on the inside which is really the self-soul that they truly are.

Identifying too much with ourselves physically, with the world in which we live or materialism, is fleeting, it's temporary, we didn't come with it and we don't leave with it, but we leave with what we gain inside of our heart, inside of ourselves.

I would direct someone to realise that they cannot lose, they cannot fully lose that self, so when things are ripped away completely, to see it as a spiritual process. It's one that says you're off path, it's time to take stock and begin afresh, always knowing that they can begin afresh and that we can begin many times in life so long as we recognise those moments.

Laura:

What would be one question that someone could ask to guide them into greater connection with their innate self?

Yasmeen:

I would ask them what feels right for you in this moment, and to absolutely trust what answers inside of them, if their mind jumps in and tries to work it out, I would encourage them to keep trying. Just pause, take a breath, and ask what feels right for you in this moment and to trust even the simplicity of what they feel answers inside of them.

People may answer, "I just need to rest." So often they'll realise that they've had this message from within themselves and they haven't trusted it because life says, "No. I'm busy." or " I have to do this or keep going." Their whole being is saying, "Can you just pause, can you just take a breath, can you rest?"

That and giving permission to listen to and trust that voice inside, in the rest they begin to recover, they begin to restore themselves and they start realising what really matters. That's not easy, some people are very invested in the physical lives that they're living and have created but they begin to become more self-aware, recognising their spirituality, perhaps their values, and just beginning to look at that.

So, some people end up with epiphany where they just sell everything up and go and live somewhere very simply in a very small way and their focus becomes really about focusing on what spiritually matters to them, but I really invite people to really feel what do you most need, what is right for you and to trust that answer because it's never wrong.

Laura:

Is there anything else you or Raman feel called to share?

Yasmeen:

Raman's immediately saying that at this particular time as we move into a transition and awakening there are many souls who are deciding to leave, and it will be immensely disturbing for all of us as we see this happen.

There are some souls who have been living disconnected for so long that it becomes immensely unbearable and they're not yet seeing hope in the world. But he says that as we all start to recognise our humanity, how we are the same, no matter where we are from, we will start to feel more people reaching out, will begin to recognise when others are not doing so well and will make more effort to connect.

He says this is a huge transition because we get very singularly focused on ourselves, on what we need, and yet we're going to recognise that we need each other, we need to feel those connections we have with each other and how much we are better when we feel that exchange of energy or love.

So, we're going to start to see what's missing and from that the answers will come. So, we're doing it mentally at the moment and a lot of studies are being done and they're recognising what's causing what is quite a huge epidemic in our world but we're also going to start to feel what the answer is, and it isn't medication.

It is really that love and care that we need to grow and thrive and that's the future, it will come he says but we're not quite there. We're leading there, we're getting there but right now there's so much we can do for ourselves to reach out if we're honest in our need, to talk with others, and not feel ashamed, not feel that we're failing, to really realise that life isn't beautiful without that connection.

Laura:

Why are so many of our youth committing suicide?

Yasmeen:

Because there are not many ways or places that the young can feel able to be their true self and express how they feel. They end up feeling disconnected from themselves, from others and sources of support. When this becomes too painful or the medication they are taking removes them further from feeling they fit or can join society, they want to stop the feelings and pain.

The world has become a place of fast paced consumerism. The young struggle to participate or even want to and it does not meet their needs. We do need to examine our values and change the way we measure worth in human beings and their contribution, beyond monetary value.

Raman has shown me much about what has been affecting our young people of all ages. Our collective needs connection and a sense of belonging.

Laura:

What is the true silent killer?

Yasmeen:

Lack of love. Yes, love is undeniably the force of the Universe and the force of creation. It is what we are part of, and is what we return to. It is what is manifest in so many beautiful ways in this world.

> *Yasmeen Clark is the Founder and Director of Pascha Therapies Ltd*
> *Channel and Medium for Raman Pascha Persian Spiritual Master*
> *President of the The New Zealand Association of Intuitive & Pascha*
> *Therapists Principal Teacher of Pascha Therapy Training*

For more info:

http://www.pascha.co.nz/

ANNIE

*W*hen my mom, Annie, suddenly passed away in August 2019 I had just started a home renovation- one that I did not feel like I could continue after her death because I was deep in grief. I felt like someone had ripped out my heart when she left our earth, it was so unexpected.

Simple things like getting up in the morning was a hard task. As the days went on I knew I had to complete the project I had started, not just for myself but I had investors I was responsible for, and of course I knew my Mom would have wanted me to, afterall she had the best sense of design and I believe my creativity and interest in interior design was a gift from her.

After months of hard work, the house was done. I staged it to sell, with all the details my mom would have loved- beautiful white orchids in the entry surrounded by rose quartz to bring in all of the love and good energy.

On the final day of clean up, I got up that morning and prayed hard and asked my mom to show me a sign that she was with me and had been a part of this project. I felt like I hadn't felt her presence in a while and I missed her terribly.

I got to the house and my favorite guy on our construction crew was there early by himself, up on the roof, cleaning it off. I called up to him to say hi and when he turned around I almost lost my breath… he was wearing an "Annie" t-shirt!!! My mom's name was Annie!

Now this may seem like a coincidence, but I know it was a sign from her. You see, Marco (the construction worker) had worn the exact same black sweatshirt every day on the job. Maybe he had also worn the Annie t-shirt underneath it every day-- but the day I had asked for my mom to say hi -- there it was loud and clear! I was overjoyed to get such a beautiful hello and greeting from my mom!

Gratitude to Bettina Bell for sharing her story.

CATHERINE

*M*y life has been and continues to be backfilled with so much love and has been beyond miraculous.

I believe my past wife Catherine has had a direct hand in all of it.

Everything in my story is true.

May you receive a little of the faith and grace I have received!

Catherine, thank you again for the adventure and for the life we have shared.

The Fox...

After Catherine and I had been dating a while I invited her to Evergreen to stay at our place there with my family and celebrate the 4th of July. I was already head over heels in love with her, but she was not quite there and had some lingering baggage from her previous relationship.

We decided to sleep under the stars on the first night in Evergreen. At first light a red fox approached our bedding and encircled us one time and quietly walked away into the forest, such a magical moment!

Later that day, Catherine professed her love for me for the first time.

Many years later, Catherine passed in the same house, and again at first light of that day, when I walked down to the cabin by myself, a fox appeared, paused and looked at me before walking softly into the forest.

Bagpipes and Blue Skies

When Catherine and I started dating, the first concert we saw together was The Allman Brothers Band at Red Rocks. We had a great time at that show and the band seemed to follow us around for a while. We saw them in Telluride and Aspen and at Red Rocks again. They became our band. We got to see them live 7 times. We used to sing along to a lot of their songs, but especially Blue Sky, "You're my sunshine, you're my sunny day, don't you know it makes me smile when you turn your love my way." That was our song and we used to laugh when we sang it to each other.

After we had been married for about 10 years, Catherine and I decided to head to the southwest and drive to Laughlin, Nevada for an unconventional Christmas adventure. We stayed at a golf resort called Avi Resort, an Indian casino about 10 miles off the main drag in Laughlin. It was a great spot on the river, a nice golf course and it was far from the other casinos. We had a great time and a very memorable holiday vacation.

In the months leading up to Catherine's passing, we had to have these difficult conversations about what to do after and last wishes, etc. not a great time, let me tell you.

One of the things that Catherine insisted on was to have bagpipes played at her memorial. She wanted to have someone to play Amazing Grace at some point during the service. I was lucky enough to have a dear friend of mine that is a very accomplished bagpipe player, and he was honored to oblige.

September 2015, 10 days after Catherine died, I needed some time to myself to process everything. I decided to rent a car and start driving. I headed south west with a general idea of going back to where she and I had started our journey together. I had my golf clubs, my camera and fishing gear in case the moment or location moved me.

I was grieving, and I cried a lot on that trip. I also listened to books on tape and good music to soothe my soul.

During the drive there were moments I could feel Catherine was with me. In fact most of the time I felt like she was still my co-pilot, sitting in the passenger seat next to me. I think most people going through that feel a presence, especially around the time of passing.

After the first week, after leaving Sedona, AZ I headed to Laughlin, Nevada. I found a hotel suite overlooking the Colorado River. That evening I went downstairs and sat down at the blackjack table and started chatting with the other players at the table.

One of them, an older gentleman, was agitated because his buddy was standing him up on a round of golf the next day, he had a tee time booked for 2 pm. I mentioned that I may be able to play, and he was excited to invite me!

The man said we were going to play at a place called Avi. There are a lot of courses in that area, so I was a little surprised to hear that. I said, "Avi? Yea, I know that place, I have been there before," remembering my trip with Catherine. This was going to be fun and serendipitous!

As I drove along the way to the Avi Resort, I tuned in to a local radio station, and after a few songs, the station reminded me of a station Catherine and I used to listen to in Denver, KBCO, an adult alternative mix mostly.

I was listening to the music and getting a bit lost as things had built up a lot since I was last there! A few more songs played as I made my way there, mostly classics with some newer stuff, and one song was ending as I pulled into the parking lot.

Then as I am rolling into the parking lot, out of the blue the station starts playing "Amazing Grace on the Bagpipes"!!!! I burst into tears and had to find a parking spot fast, as I sat there for 10 minutes sheading both tears of joy. I also felt so overwhelmed with still missing her and wanting to grab her for playing this trick on me! She knows you are not supposed to be late to tee time!

I finally got my act together and met up with Jim, the man who invited me to join him. We had a nice round of golf, and I said my goodbyes to Jim in the parking lot and we both went back to our cars. I threw my clubs in the trunk, changed my shoes, and sat down in the car, and reflected on what a crazy thing that was with the bagpipes song! Wow, what a sign, without a doubt with that kind of timing?

I am spiritual, but often skeptical too, so I was trying to be open to other "possibilities." I turned the car on to leave, and the radio came on and the music started right from the beginning, as if it were cued up to play "Blue Skies" by The Allman Brothers Band.

This is ALL a true story. I sat in the car again and cried those bittersweet tears of joy.

I made the drive back to Denver from Laughlin and cried those bittersweet tears along the way and reflected on what had occurred at the golf course and it was still hard to believe it happened.

Was it simply a coincidence? I tried to do some basic probability equations, I am not a math major, BUT I did find the odds to be astronomical that those things happened at those exact moments at that specific place in time and space. They say timing is everything and that is true, the message was received, right on time.

Over the next several weeks I continued some progress through grieving and preparing myself to return to our Mexico home. The "space" was the most challenging thing for me to navigate, a huge part of my life was gone, there was a profound feeling of so much empty space. I had always had her on my mind, I did not realize how much of my attention it held. It truly felt like floating through life for a while.

Thinking about her, being gone was sad, but the space was a possibility. I came around to that and I found Catherine in that space too, as a gentle or sometimes dramatic guide.

Not long before returning to Mexico, the next big sign I received was driving back from a poker tournament with a dear friend of mine. We had dinner before the tournament and talked about Catherine of course and how I was doing and we also said we are going to win the poker tournament and finish 1st and 2nd!

We ended up with just under 100 players in the tournament that night, and sure enough I won the tournament and my friend got second. I believe Catherine definitely had a hand in our winning hands!

On the way home, I started thinking about the cute waitress at the casino, who was bringing me iced tea all night. I had seen her there before on previous nights, but did not take much interest, other than noting she was attractive, and I liked her upbeat positive attitude.

As I am driving through the canyon road back home in the early morning hours, I am daydreaming in the space of possibilities, and I start thinking about that girl in the casino again, maybe I should ask her out?

As the thought is passing through my mind, I hear Catherine's voice from the back seat of the car..."WAIT". Just one word, but clear as if she were sitting right behind me.

A couple weeks after that I decided it was time to return to Tulum. The messages continued in Tulum as I began to rebuild my life, still floating in that space, but moving through it and trying to stay busy doing something. I decided it would be a good time to make some changes in the house and started working on making the space for me.

Uncharacteristically out of season, I started seeing blue butterflies everywhere, in my house, landing on me, following me and generally around all the time! I included some butterflies in the redecorations around the house and was trying to accept the whole transformation process. The butterflies were a nice touch and showed up again.

A few months before Catherine passed away, I had an immensely powerful dream of an image with my hand laying on a full pregnant belly. It was a little disturbing, Catherine and I did not have children and I was past that, at almost 50 years old.

I was uncomfortable with the dream and I did not share it with Catherine, it was seemingly out of the blue, but it was powerful, and it stayed with me.

A few months after returning to Tulum, I ventured back into dating as an emotionally unavailable person. I wanted to have some companionship - I missed that. I met a waitress at a place I frequented, yea I know, what a cliché. What can I say, she was cute, young and single, and she seemed to like me too!

This was a casual affair! Erika and I were good for each other at that time, she had also just come out of a relationship that was dying, we were both grieving our losses and were not interested in anything remotely serious.

We carried on in our casual affair for several months and it was nice.

Sometime around 3-4 months into our relationship, I started noticing my feelings towards her change. I held back my emotions a bit, how could I be having these feelings so soon? Weeks passed and I wondered if she was feeling it too. It was not long after that I expressed my feelings to her and she was feeling it too, love was back. Did I mention she also had a tattoo of a blue butterfly on her left hip?

We had a trip planned to meet up with some of my friends in Baja for an annual fishing trip. We had a great time meeting up there for a few days before parting ways for the summer, as I was heading back to Colorado. Erika also wanted to have some time and space too, we both wanted to have some space with these new strong feelings about each other. It was true, we did love each other and missed each other in the weeks apart.

Upon my return to Tulum, Erika was acting odd. She had picked me up from the bus station after I got back from the airport and she was quiet. We made small talk about the trip for a while on the drive back, before I asked her, what is going on? You seem like you want to tell me something... after a long pause she said she wanted to wait till we got home, BUT she would tell me now, she was pregnant! We were going to have a baby! To say I was shocked is an understatement, but I did later see my hand laying on a belly full of a new life and his name is Nico.

Gratitude to Ron Burdine *for sharing his story and to our beloved Catherine.....
for all of your continued support.*

ron@mexicoonmymind.com

DIVINE ASSIGNMENT

*W*hen our loved ones die suddenly and dramatically, we are often left feeling a sense of shame, guilt, and regret for all of the things we wished we *could have* said, and perhaps for the things we wish we *hadn't* said.

If you are feeling a need for closure with a loved one who has taken their life, died in a sudden manner, or has passed away leaving you with a feeling of remorse and/or incompletion, this divine assignment will be incredibly supportive.

This is an opportunity for a transdimensional connection, and can offer you a sense of closure and/or a new beginning with your loved one. It is very nourishing for your emotional well being, and your ability to move on, to create something new and beautiful for your life.

This transformational assignment will allow you a chance to reclaim the energies that have been hijacked by any feelings of regret or incompletion. This will in turn allow you to become vibrationally harmonious and therefore emotionally available for continued connection, if you so choose.

'Divine Assignment Ritual / Ceremony'
Aligning your intention with action

What is needed:

- Your intention
- Supportive environment
- Piece of paper
- Something to write with
- Candle

Find a quiet place where you can freely express yourself.

Light a candle and take three deep breaths.

State your Intention:

You can allow your intuition to inform your intention for this ritual, however it is important that the focus of what you desire feels life affirming to you.

Some questions to promote your clarity:

- What would you like to feel when this ceremony/ritual is complete?

- Would you like a sense of closure and completion with your loved one?

- Would you like to continue to feel their presence in your life and cultivate a new relating dynamic?

Examples of intention:

- I am gifting myself an opportunity to be liberated and allow for something nurturing and beautiful to come from this experience.

- I am inviting an opportunity to commune and connect with my loved one, so they may hear my peace.

- I am sharing for the purpose of closure and completion for that aspect of my past.

- I am open to a mutually beneficial connection to continue with my loved one, so that I may continue to receive their guidance and to feel their love.

Once you are clear, glow ahead and state your intention aloud.

My intention for this divine assignment is to _____.

Ask your loved one to lay their prayers down next to yours, for the benefit of all.

Imagination:

Imagine that you have a direct line to your beloved, who is now in Spirit form. They are receptive to you and your heart-core intention.

You can close your eyes and imagine you are sitting across from them, or whatever imaginings evokes a feeling that you are speaking directly to them and they are listening.

What would you like to share with them?

- What would you like them to know now?

- What does your heart need to share so that you can be free from this?

Inspired Action:

Have your piece of paper and pen handy. Begin to write down what arises. (You can also speak it aloud, depending on what tools you have available to you. The most important element is your intention partnered with your action).

Allow yourself to freely express, as it is important to release any emotions,

Express your stream of consciousness through the profound catalyst of the written word.

You may find it helpful to have some music playing to assist in this process.

As you begin to write, it is vital to have the discernment that you are not dwelling in the past and activating lower vibrational energies of victimization. You will know if this is happening based on your emotional guidance system.

This is your opportunity to utilize the perceived 'loss' of your loved one as an opportunity to liberate yourself and 'gain' a continued connection going forward if this serves your journey. Or you may decide to come into conscious completion.

When your divine assignment is complete, you will be feeling lighter and more expansive, perhaps even mixed with feelings of relief and love.

Once you feel complete with your share, you can also burn what you have written and allow the fires of transformation to illuminate for you how everything changes form in the ultimate recycling program of 'energy'. (Be cautious about your burning of this).

Once this has occurred you can speak aloud - I am complete with this Divine Assignment.

As Rumi once said, 'Don't grieve. Everything you lose comes around in a different form."

This assignment will allow you to be present for all of the de*light*ful ways that your loved one will choose to communicate their love and presence to you going forward.

EPILOGUE

ear Fellow Traveler,

Thank you for joining me on your journey of remembrance. It has been a sincere honor to serve you. This is my blessing for you as you continue your journey~

May you trust yourSelf and know your knowing.

May you trust in the divine unfoldment and sacred intention for your journey.

May you always remember that Source is flowing through you, *as you*.

May you continue to be an instrument for beauty, love, light and compassion.

May you walk the Beauty Way as the embodiment of pure consciousness, resilient in your soul's worth.

May you be grounded in humility for those that have come before and in reverence of those that are coming.

May you walk with your head held high and your heart open, anchored in the conviction of your eternal worth and value, and unified with all of creation.

May *trust* be your benefactor and *Source* your source.

With love as your instrument, your life becomes your blessing.

Your journey, a love story for the ages.

NEXT STEP'S ON YOUR JOURNEY

Join '**The JOURNEY BACK TO SELF Book Club**' to share thoughts and inspirations from the book, connect with other readers, receive inspiration from Laura, and updates on '*Journey Back To Self*' events!

https://www.facebook.com/groups/331904338633909

Join **The Sanctuary of Vulnerability**

https://www.facebook.com/groups/899016277381726

This is a private Facebook group where you can be held in a community of compassion, to share without shame and to connect with people who can relate to what you are going through. If you have lost a loved one to suicide, this is a place where you can come to honor your loved one. JOIN US!

It is time to bank on our greatest resource- the human heart and the human Spirit. Together we rise.

ABOUT THE AUTHOR

Laura Fredrickson is an Empowerment Specialist, Soul Whisperer, International Speaker and Best Selling Author. For over 20 years, Laura's global mission is to empower people to remember their self worth and innate value and their signature significance to this planet.

The loss of Laura's parents to a dual suicide, as well as her own brush with suicide after losing everything in the tech collapse, were catalysts for Laura to redefine her life and sense of identity, and ultimately informed her purpose to guide others who had lost their way.

Laura has enriched the lives of thousands of people to include Victoria Secret Supermodels, Celebrities, UN Ambassadors, and global leaders and has served as a trusted advisor for executives and companies who are seeking to shift their challenges and setbacks into growth opportunities.

Laura Fredrickson possesses a rare blend of natural talent, unique expertise, personal story and wisdom and has presented at events in company with Richard Branson, Tim Ferriss, Tony Hsieh and Gabby Bernstein. Laura is revered as one of the most up and coming spiritual leaders of our time.

In love and service,

Laura

To continue your journey with Laura, please connect with her here:

www.laurafredrickson.com

ACKNOWLEDGEMENTS

*D*eep gratitude for all of my ancestors who have laid their prayers down next to mine, and to all of the persistent beings of love and light that have always guided me back to the truth of who I am, during what often felt like the impenetrable pitch black night of my soul.

Thank you to Spirit and the Divine Conspiracy who have always organized impeccably for the Highest outcome.

Thank you to Lorcan O'Toole for being the catalyst for the vision of this book to be known and felt by me.

My heart overflows with appreciation for these embodied angels that offered the refuge of love and support when I needed it the most- Benjamin Phelan, Auntie Linda, Jan Salerno, Heather Brand of Shloaka, Jessie Morgan, Jill Jackson, and Vassa Neimark.

Thank you to all that shared their wisdom in the Innerviews.

"Matur Suksma" and "Terima Kasih" to Mama Bali for holding me so deeply in your embrace, always reminding me of the undercurrent of well being. The grace of your people, land and all of Her inhabitants have nourished me more than words can express.

Thank you to Mother Earth for the incredible honor you have bestowed to me, allowing me to incarnate here and partake in this magical and awe-full journey here.

Last but not least, I am grateful to mySelf. This immense journey I have embarked on has not been easy, but worth every step.

Made in the USA
Las Vegas, NV
21 October 2021

32768660R00118